PRICE GUIDE

W9-AXD-365

AMERICAS, AUSTRALIA & PACIFIC ISLANDS COSTUMED DOLLS

BY POLLY & PAM JUDD

3rd in Series

Published by Hobby House Press

Hobby House Press, Inc.
Grantsville, Maryland 21536

DEDICATION

The authors dedicate this book to the many doll clubs around the world. We wish to thank our own clubs, the Cleveland Doll Club, the Northern Ohio Doll Club and the After Dark Doll Study Club of Ohio, for the fellowship, knowledge and just plain fun we have shared with the members. We also dedicate it to Eryn and Kyle Judd as they complete their college years and enter the Communications Field.

ACKNOWLEDGEMENTS

The authors wish to thank the following people for their contributions to this book:
Sherry Morgan for pictures of her international dolls, Kathy Koliha for Hawaiian dolls; Jean Francis, who will always be the "Doll Lady of Canada" to us; Lois Janner, the "Doll Lady of Cleveland"; Laura Brown; Joseph Colembieski; Barbara and Jim Comienski; Crossford Trading Company; Sandi Dodd; Beverley Findlay; Penny Hadfield; Jean Horton; Kathy Lincoln; Helene Marlowe; Mary Merritt Doll Museum; Pat Parton; Dee Percefull; Thelma Purvis; Louise Schnell; Betsy Toft; Tradewind Auction Gallery; Betty Velican; and Buddy Wheet, Shirley Karaba and Sandy Strater who share our dolls and travel. We don't leave home without them.

Finally, we cannot heap enough praise on our editors Mary Beth Ruddell and John Axe.

FRONT COVER: *Left to Right:* **Venezuelan Girl Dancing the Yarn Dance.** *See page 145 for more information.* **Piu Skirt Dolls.** *See page 12 for more information.* **Hawaiian Children.** *See page 109 for more information.*
TITLE PAGE: Hawaiian Children. *See pages 1 and 109 for more information.*
BACK COVER: Brazilian Girl and Boy. *See page 127 for more information.*

Additional copies of this book may be purchased at $14.95 (plus postage and handling) from
Hobby House Press, Inc.
1 Corporate Drive
Grantsville, Maryland 21536
1-800-554-1447
or from your favorite bookstore or dealer.

©1997 Pam & Polly Judd

Printed in the United States of America.

ISBN: 0-87588-472-5

TABLE OF CONTENTS

PREFACE

"Aloha" means both hello and goodbye. We welcome you to the third book in the trilogy of books about doll costumes around the world. For the authors it has been a grand tour.

This book covers many miles of both continental lands and islands. Each country is different, and the people have adapted their natural resources to their clothes and dolls. These resources range from tapa cloth in the South Pacific islands to fur in the Arctic. It shows us that people can survive, be comfortable and enjoy life in their world. The dolls also help us understand these concepts. It has been a wonderful voyage both through research and through our own world travels. We wish you "Bon Voyage" and "Aloha".

Polly and Pam Judd

SYSTEM USED FOR PRICING DOLLS

During our travels around the country and through our mail we have seen increased interest in identifying the doll costumes of the people of the world. There is a strong market for International dolls in their original condition, clothes, and if possible in their original boxes.

In researching this book, we found that Native American dolls and Native Canadian dolls are of particular interest, and the prices have been soaring. At an Ohio auction an old Sioux Indian doll was gaveled down for $2,900 (see *Illustration 136*). The Kachina dolls have always been very popular as well as the carved wooden dolls from such places as New Guinea.

As stated in Book 2, Kimport dolls and other dolls from various international mail order houses of the 1930s to the 1950s are eagerly sought and are increasing in value.

Prices were gathered from many sources from various parts of the United States. In this book the price range of dolls covers "good to tissue-mint-in-box." Dolls in poor condition will be about one third to one half of the lowest price.

The dolls in this book are different from those in many other books. While most of them cannot be called rare dolls, they have a way of increasing in value as they are identified and people understand their place in history.

AUSTRALIA

Australia is the world's smallest continent. Much of the land is a harsh desert called an "outback"; however, the people are hard working, fun and sports-loving.

Australia includes six states, the Northern Territory and the Australian Capital Territory. The six states are Western Australia, Queensland, South Australia, New South Wales, Victoria, and Tasmania.

The original inhabitants of Australia are the aborigines who have lived there for thousands of years.

Australia was settled by the English who sent prisoners there in the 18th century. Since 1945 people from other parts of the world also settled. Australia's dolls reflect this heritage.

Like other people around the world, Australians have a growing interest in dolls and doll collecting. They have doll museums, clubs, magazines, books, doll companies, and artists who make both native and play dolls. Their stuffed animals, such as kangaroos, koalas, and sheep are fun additions to collections worldwide.

1. Widgeon, a Lubra Aborigine in the Australian Outback: 12in (31cm); cloth; painted face; mohair wig; shell, seed necklace; 1950. Two live kangaroos are in the background, Kimport imported some of these dolls.
MARKS: "WIDGEON A LUBRA//WALLABY FUR SKIRT//SHELLS AND SEEDS FROM MAGNETIC IS. NO."

1

2. *Left to Right:* **English Man Criminal Sent to Australia as Penalty:** 7.5in (18cm); all vinyl; white prisoner hat (like a cook's hat); white flour sack convict suit with black arrows; red tie; wool gray beard; painted face; ball and chain on left foot; carrying a stick with a black iron block.

MARKS: His leaflet says, "Hello I am Arthur No. 136. I was sentenced to the Penal Colony of Australia with the first fleet for stealing in 1788. The voyage was very cruel with little food, water, and filthy conditions. Many died. After committing further offenses on arrival, it was hard labor building roads and dwellings. We are called 'Iron Gangs'." His plastic container says "Kooch//Kou Souvenirs."

English Woman Criminal Sent to Australia: 7.5in (18cm); vinyl; white mob cap; pink fringed scarf; dress and apron made of flour sacks: carries wool duster; ball and chain attached to her left ankle; 1989.

MARKS: "Australian//made" printed over outline of boomerang on body. A leaflet says, "Hello! I'm Mary Ann No. 31. I was transported to the Penal Colony of Australia at the age of 16 for stealing a pound of butter. While serving my 7 year sentence, I was given a 'ticket of leave' which allowed me to work on a farm. Later I made an application and was granted permission to marry a free man." Her plastic container says "Kooch//Kou Souvenirs."

3. *Left to Right:* **Koala Dressed as a Swagman:** 8in (20cm); stuffed mock fur body; plastic eyes and nose; brown felt swagman-type hat with small corks which bob as he walks through the bush, scattering mosquitoes; purchased in Australia. For more information about Swagman see *Illustration 4*.
MARKS: None.

Budgerree Doll (Aborigine Warrior Chief): 14in (36cm) body made of shiny, stuffed black cotton; hand painted decorations in maroon, yellow, white; straw breechcloth; straw decorations at ankles; carrying a long sword and carved boomerang with decorations.

The boomerang is a curved piece of wood which when thrown returns to the thrower. The aborigine warrior was very skilled with this method of waging war on the enemy.
MARKS: "The Sarah Midgley// Budgerree Doll//Copyright 11523" on tag. "Kimport" tag also.

Kangaroo with a Baby in her Pouch: 12in (31cm); stuffed mock fur body; orange ribbon around neck of mother and baby; purchased in Australia.
MARKS: None.

"Waltzing Matilda" is a song about an itinerant bush worker who "waltzes" across the harsh, dry heartland of Australia looking for work and accepting what is available with unserved grace. He calls his backpack "Matilda" and sings as he travels. He symbolizes freedom, ingenuity, self-reliance, all qualities which the Australians cherish. ("Waltzing Matilda" is considered the unofficial "national anthem" of Australia.)

Each doll, a "Swagman," carries a bedroll with his possessions on his back. Their white "tucker" around the neck contains flour, tea, game killed, and any food they can beg, borrow, steal or work for on a farm, or "station," in the outback. Cork "bobs" hang from their Australian hats to keep off black flies. They carry a "Billy" bucket in which they cook food and boil tea. Each has a diamond patch on their left pant leg.

4

4. *Left to Right:* **Three Swaggies:** 9.5in (23cm), 9.5in (23cm), 7in (18cm). The middle "Swaggie" is standing on a music box which plays "Waltzing Matilda," written by bush poet A. B. Paterson. The doll on the left has a papier-mâché head; the doll in the middle has a hard plastic head; the doll on the right has a celluloid head and arms; all have cloth bodies.
MARKS: "Original by Selma West" on doll on left. Others not marked.

5. **Early Settler of Australia:** 7in (18cm); hard plastic body; Australian-style hat; patchwork dress; white apron; carries mop.

The doll represents an early settler who came to Australia. Since she is a servant, she probably is a bonded servant. However, she could also have been a criminal from England who has served her sentence and now is trying to start a new life.
MARKS: None.

5

6. Aboriginal Couple from Australia: 13in (33cm); black satin bodies; molded faces; bushy, curly hair; the woman's skirt has delicate emu feathers; the waistband is decorated with tiny seashells; matching necklace; the man has brick red ochre and white painting; his headdress has emu feathers; fabric covered with rough fiber is used for the loincloth of the man; a wooden boomerang is in the left hand; he has a carved spear in the right hand; 1940s-1950s.
MARKS: "The Sarah Midgley//Budgenee Doll//reg 71899//copyright 15775//" on tag. *Helene Marlowe Collection.*

Kimport advertised these dolls in *Doll News,* November-December, 1956.

6

7. Bindi: 14in (36cm); vinyl; jointed arms and legs; bushy hair; cloth wrap-around red skirt; 1960s. (The doll is designed to represent an aboriginal. The company was sold to the Netta Company in 1976. The doll was remolded with a closed mouth in 1992.)
MARKS: "Metti. Adelaide, South Australia." *Thelma Purvis Collection.*

7

8. Aboriginal: 8in (20cm); black hard plastic; light brown cotton hair, eyebrows, beard; white design painted on body, arms, legs; multi-colored cotton skirt; wood burned design on shield; long walking stick; 1970s-1990s. <u>**MARKS**</u>**:** "Australian Aboriginal//Made in Australia" sign on base.

8

When the first Western explorers discovered New Zealand in the late 18th century, they found the Maori people who are believed to have migrated by boat from the eastern Pacific. They had some difficulties with the early white settlers, but after minor wars, they soon adapted to the European ways.

Today the Maori people are citizens of New Zealand. They have integrated well, but like other citizens they cherish their past and teach their children the heritage and art of the early days.

The dolls in this book are dressed in colorful costumes which in yesteryear were handmade with materials from New Zealand's islands.

9

9. *Left:* **Maori Mother and Baby:** 5in (13cm) hard plastic Baby; 8in (20cm); Baby is undressed; vinyl Mother is dressed in a traditional costume and is barefoot; Parr Company, 1989.

Right: **Maori Dancer:** 21in (53cm); vinyl; sleep eyes; dressed in complete, traditional costume; poise balls of dancer; feathered cape well preserved; exceptional doll; maker unknown; early 1980s.

The Parr Company of Australia tried to make each doll an educational toy. The box in the picture shows a New Zealand flag, map, picture of a Maori compound, and essential information about New Zealand.

A card came in the box with the following costume identification.

KAKAHU

The Clothes of the Maori

"The dressing of the Maori was an intricate handcraft, with differing designs according to the tribe. Personal adornments consisted of bone, greenstone (jade); art of Moko (carving of the face), which was peculiar to the N.Z. Maori.

"The Hei-Tiki or Tiki, a greenstone symbol of fertility worn around the neck, was priced and handed from generation to generation. Greenstone and bone earrings are also worn.

"The head bands and bodices were woven in different patterns and designs according to the tribe. The piu piu, skirts made of flax, were carefully scraped to form a pattern, then dyed in the mud pools.

"Cloaks were made of various materials according to climate and ranking in the tribe. Dog hair, wood, pigeon feathers and flax (for wet weather) were used. Full Kiwi bird feather cloaks, which took many months to make, were worn by chiefs only.

"Poi balls, made of flax, were originally used by warriors to keep their wrists supple for battle. Now wahines (females) and warriors use them for actions in songs which tell their history. The spear, commonly used by warriors, is called a taiaha."

MARKS: None.

10. Maori Toddler Hemi: 14.5in (37cm) all brown bisque; jointed at hips, shoulders; socket head; large brown glass eyes; dimples in cheeks; painted facial features; brown, acrylic wig; wears greenstone (tiki) necklace; Maori flax shirt; flax kilt (piupiu); 1993.

Tiki was the first man in Maori folklore, and the carved stone is usually passed down from generation to generation as it gives "mana" (spirit power) to the new wearer.

The doll was made by Janis Harris, a New Zealand doll artist.

Sherry Morgan Collection.

10

11. *Left to Right:* **Wahine:** 7in (18cm); vinyl; hand woven (bodia) headband; feather cloak; genuine greenstone titki; pui pui skirt; feather cloak; packaged in a carton; from 1986 catalog.

Warrior: 7in (18cm) vinyl; wooden spear; feather cloak; (piu piu) skirt; genuine greenstone (tiki); handwoven strap; earring; packaged in carton; from 1986 catalog.
MARKS: Unknown.
From Crossford Trading Co. Ltd. catalog.

11

12. Piu Skirt Dolls: Vinyl; dressed in girl's and women's Maori Costumes; the more expensive ones are wearing feather cloaks; 1986.
<u>MARKS:</u> Unknown.
From Crossford Trading Co. Ltd. catalog.

12

13

13. *Left to Right:* **Pania:** 7in (18cm); vinyl doll; sitting on revolving musical stand; dancing costume; headband; piu piu skirt; 1986.
<u>MARKS:</u> None.
From Crossford Trading Co. Ltd. catalog.

Authentic Wahine: Vinyl doll; 11in (28cm); standing on revolving musical stand; hand woven headband; bodice (piu piu) skirt; (raupo poise) greenstone; tiki and earring; feather cloak and shin molo; 1986.
<u>MARKS:</u> None.
From Crossford Trading Co. Ltd. catalog.

14. Mira Maoriland's Maid: 15.5in (39cm); composition head; cloth body; painted face; mohair wig; light brown skin; fringed red cotton dress with white stripe in skirt; greenstone necklace (tiki); dyed flax piu piu (dance kilt); kakahy (flax cloak) with a few feathers left woven into it; attached in back is a flax ball (poi) used for the famous Maori dance; 1930s.
MARKS: "Mira Maoriland's Maid."

15. Authentic Wahine Dancer: 6in (15cm); cloth body except for pottery arms; greenstone (tiki); red and white patterned bodice; handwoven headband (tipare); red skirt; white dyed wool (piu piu) dance kilt; gold braid on sleeves; 1959.
MARKS: "Handcrafted for Klylo" tag.
Thelma Purvis Collection.

ANTIGUA

Antigua is an island in the Leeward Island Group of the Lesser Antilles of the Caribbean Sea. Since 1981 it has been part of the nation of Antigua and Barbuda.

16. Fruit Peddler: 11in (28cm); black rayon body; red cotton multicolored dress; tan woven basket on her head carrying molded fruit; gold hoop earrings; 1995.
MARKS: "ANTIGUA" embroidered on it.

16

ARUBA

Aruba is a Dutch semi-arid island in the Lesser Antilles near the South American coast. Visitors find legendary beaches, Dutch cuisine, and picturesque windmills powered by the trade winds.

17. Fruit Peddler: 9in (23cm); cloth body; white apron and skirt; blue blouse; red bandana; carrying handwoven basket with artificial fruit.
MARKS: "ARUBA" written on band of apron.
Beverley Findlay Collection.

17

BAHAMAS

A short hop from Miami, the sunny Bahamas have greeted visitors for many years. There they find a British tradition, tropical sunshine, beaches, resorts, casinos, and golf courses. Among the 22 inhabited islands are Paradise Island, Grand Bahama Island, Great Abaco, Eleuthera, and New Providence Island. Each features fun for everyone watched over by the British "Bobby" in Bermuda shorts. The many dolls are fun, too. Although there are several styles, the "Bobby" has captured the attention of doll collectors for many years.

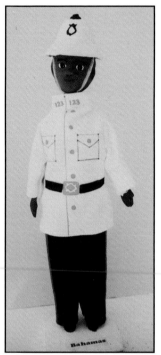

18

18. Abaco Island Bahamas Policeman: 11.75in (30cm); painted body; black cotton pants with red felt stripes; yellow lithographed belt buckle.
MARKS: "Bahamas" sticker on base; Caribbean Production Ltd; Nassau, Bahamas.
Sherry Morgan Collection.

19. *Left to Right:* **Rafia Clown:** 16in (41cm); black cloth head; body made of green raffia; vivid green, brown, white, red, and yellow clown costume; woven straw hat and shoes; unknown date.
MARKS: "BAHAMAS" sewn with red raffia on hat.

Bermuda Policeman: 8in (20cm); all hard plastic; jointed at shoulders, head, hips; sleep eyes; hard plastic hat; molded blue high shoes; light blue cotton shirt with gold buttons; dark blue knee-length pants with black belt and silver buckle; doll stands alone; 1950s.
MARKS: "BERMUDA" gold seal on back of pants; "Made in England" seal on bottom of shoe.

19

BARBADOS

Barbados was a British island in the Windward Islands chain of the West Indies group in the Caribbean Sea from the 1620s until it became independent in 1966. Along with beaches and balmy breezes, it also has historic churches, plantations, and the original Trafalgar Square constructed 17 years before the one in England.

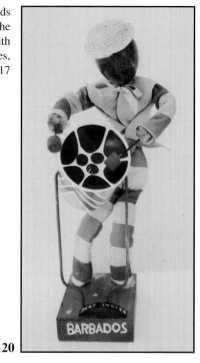

20. Man Playing Steel Drum: Wooden head; cord body over wire; multi-colored jump suit; pink sash; straw hat; 1972.
Sherry Morgan Collection.

20

BERMUDA

Bermuda is in the Atlantic Ocean off the Carolina coast. Breezes are comfortable and sports, such as tennis and golf, tempt vacationers. Owned by England, there are British pubs, food and charm, and of course, genuine Bermuda policemen.

21. Bermuda Lady: 8.5in (22cm) body from bark of Bermuda tree; woven basket on head with felt oranges; red and white head scarf; burlap skirt with belt trim; red fringe around skirt; beads for facial features.
MARKS: "Made in Bermuda//for//H.& E. Smith, Ltd." tag on skirt.

21

CUBA

Columbus claimed Cuba for Spain in 1492. Today the island nation has well over 11 million people. Cuba is a Communist state and few tourists visit the island. Trade between the United States and Cuba is sparse, and few dolls except pre-Fidel Castro nightclub dolls are available.

When Fidel Castro finally reached Havana with his guerrilla fighters on January 2, 1959, American tourists were still vacationing in Cuba. At least one cruise ship was in port, and other tourists had flown to the capital for a vacation. The doll shown in *Illustration 22* was purchased by a tourist at the airport in Havana at that time. A wonderful likeness of Castro, the doll was created by the Unicos Distribuidores, C.I.D. Corporation. This information was on a hand written note inside the box.

22. Fidel Castro: 9in (23cm) soft vinyl "magic skin" in excellent condition. The uniform is well tailored with a red patch on the arm which says "26".

The doll was originally called Benipin Rebel and is dressed in the uniform of the revolutionary army.
MARKS: "Benipin Rebeldo//El símbolo de revolución triunfante//Made in Cuba" on tag. Rare doll.

22

23. Cuban Dancers: 10in (25cm); all-composition; molded and enameled with white paint; the man and the woman both wear white and red costumes; circa 1930s.
MARKS: None.

23

24. Two Dancers in Cuban Nightclub: 6.5in (17cm); floss over armature; crocheted costumes; 1950s before Fidel Castro. The man is dressed in a blue sweater and black pants with a red sash. The lady is dressed in a pink-top; a red skirt, and she has a bow in her hair.
MARKS: "Hecho en Cuba."

24

DOMINICAN REPUBLIC

The Dominican Republic shares an island in the Greater Antilles chain with Haiti. Christopher Columbus established the first European settlement in the New World at the site of the present capital, Santo Domingo. Vacationers are impressed with sophisticated hotels, nightclubs, and casinos.

25. Island Woman: 13in (33cm); clothes woven with straw and palm leaves; some strands are dyed purple and green.

This is an example of a doll made by natives of the island and it returned with a visitor many years ago. **MARKS:** "Dominican Republic" on back.

25

26. Peddler Pushing a Cart:
7.5in (19cm); molded plaster
head; armature body covered
with cotton plaid which is also
the shirt; green cardboard cap;
blue pants; 1978.
MARKS: "Dominican
Republic" and a map of the
country painted on cart.
Sherry Morgan Collection.

26

27. *Left to Right:* **Man from Puerta
Plata:** 10.5in (27cm); light brown
face, arms, legs; dried grass hair;
handmade straw hat; painted face;
blue cotton coat with yellow trim;
blue tape shoes; the doll was purchased in Puerta Plata which is an
old Spanish Port on the north
of the island.

Lady in Ribbon Dress: 6in (15cm);
vinyl head and arms; the dress is
made of the undulating weaving of
green ribbon lined with woven
wood fiber; green scarf under
unusual straw hat; 1995.
MARKS: The tag on the doll tells
that it is a souvenir of the
Dominican Republic and that it
wears a typical
costume.

27

GUADELOUPE

When a stranger steps down the gangplank of a ship anchored in Basse Terra, Guadeloupe, in the Lesser Antilles, he knows this is a different sort of Caribbean island. It is French, and the sophisticated Paris clothing, shops and restaurants can be seen nearby. The dolls are also sophisticated.

28. *Left to Right:* **Man and Woman:** 10.5in (27cm); carved, painted wood; brightly painted, elongated statues of natives; the Lady has an orange and white dress; green hat; carries a blue box on her head; blue stand. The Man wears a white shirt with red buttons and collar; yellow pants with white lines; high "crew cut" hair. He is playing a steel drum on a stand.
<u>MARKS:</u> None.   **28**

Paris Court Lady: 10in (25cm); papier-mâché drape painted in brilliant gold; 1995.
<u>MARKS:</u> None.

HAITI

Haiti shares its island in the Greater Antilles with the Dominican Republic. Due to political difficulties and poverty there have been few tourists visiting for years. However, cruise ships have started to stop in "safe" ports again. The type of dolls in *Illustration 29* have appealed to tourists in the past, and they can be found in many forms by today's collectors.

29. Peddler Dolls: Woman: 6in (15cm); cloth head over armature body; yellow armature body; yellow dress with multicolored flowers; white and red head scarf; riding carved wooden donkey with basket; 1960s.
Man: 7in (18cm); cloth over armature body; blue denim-type pants and top; yellow scarf; red polka dot head scarf; carrying sack of "Haitian Coffee Grade A"; purchased in Haiti; 1960s.
<u>**MARKS:**</u> None.

29

JAMAICA

Jamaica is the third largest island in the West Indies. It has a warm climate near the coast and a cooler climate in the inland mountains. The majority of the people are of African descent. They dress in bright colors, speak English, and are famous for their music, especially Reggae, which blends African drums and rhythms with the electric guitar. This music was especially suitable for the "limbo" dance which originated here. (see *Illustration 30*.)

The citizens have a higher rate of health and schooling than many of the other Caribbean islands. School is free through college.

Dolls from Jamaica show the colorful, musical, approach to everyday life.

30. Limbo Dancer: 6in (15cm) high; multi-colored costume; red and beige platform and limbo bar. The dancer tries to go under the bar without dislodging it or the dancer falling. The bar is lowered each time. The beat gets louder and faster until the dancer dislodges the bar; 1972.
MARKS: None.

30

31. *Left to Right:* **Traditional Jamaican Lady Doll:** 9in (23cm); hard plastic black body; yel- **31** low and black full, long skirt; ornate, ruffled apron, straw hat; carrying a basket of clay fruit on her head; 1955.
<u>MARKS</u>: None.

Mother Sitting with Baby: 7in (18cm); all cloth; felt face with pieces of felt used for eyes, nose, mouth; red, white, blue plaid blouse; kerchief on head; red felt skirt; sitting on red velvet reclining couch; all cloth baby with pieces of felt for eyes, nose, mouth; 1972.

This is a hand-crafted doll made by a local artist for the Port Antonion Craft Center.
<u>MARKS</u>: None.

Boy Playing a Ukulele: 6in (15cm); all baked clay; sculpted and painted facial features; straw hat; orange shirt; red belt; orange and white long pants; pink cloth ukulele; 1972.
<u>MARKS</u>: None.

MARTINIQUE

Martinique is a French Island whose culture features fresh bread, flowers, and sophisticated boutiques. Visitors can drive from civilization to the site of the devastation of the 1902 eruption of Mt. Peleé which changed the landscape. However, in the delightful French manner, life continues once again.

Many Africans, brought to this island as slaves, later fled to New Orleans and gave that city much of the life-style it now enjoys. Beautiful lady dolls from both places reflect this passage and represent both the island and the American city.

32.

32. *Left to Right:* **Man and Woman:** 14in (36cm); all cloth; embroidered face. 1974.
Man: Dressed in brown suit. **Woman:** Black and white check dress; white kerchief on head.
<u>MARKS</u>: None.
Thelma Purvis Collection.

Girl Dressed in Martinique Costume: 11in (28cm); black bisque head with sculptured hair; red, top and bottom of dress; inset in skirt printed with yellow and blue circles; matching red straw hat with red and yellow triangles sewn into it; 1920s and 1930s.
<u>MARKS</u>: None.
Sandra Strater Collection.

Company: Titiane, Sandra Dogué, France.

33. *Left to Right:* **Fashion Lady from Early 20th Century:** 7in (18cm); black celluloid; jointed at arms and legs; sequin earrings; thread wig in tight coils in middle of forehead and around ears; white eyelet blouse and underskirt; multi-colored plaid Madras skirt and headdress; 1960.

The booklet attached to her arm explains the costume. "I have put on my pretty embroidered chemise and fine skirt to go to the dance. On my head the Madras stretches its three tips coquettishly. They indicate I will not refuse any partner. As a jewel my best collier chou (necklace)."

Another page says, "The Sandra Dogué dolls faithfully reproduce the original costumes of Carïbe — They are produced with the greatest care and have a remarkable finish."

MARKS: "France 175 and Turtle Mark". This is the mark of Rheinische Gummi und Celluloid Fabrik Co.

33

34. All Original Martinique Fashion Lady from Early Part of the 20th Century: 13in (33cm); jointed at neck, shoulders, legs; Carton Moulé (papier-mâché) body and head; light brown skin tone; glass eyes with black pupils; dotted eyebrows; red painted lips; molded ears; yellow print dress with red, blue, purple flowers; dress is designed with a bustle effect; hand crocheted shawl and matching crocheted underskirt; second yellow underskirt to make dress stand out; painted shoes; coarse black wig; yellow and red cotton hat; the way the hat is tied determines the status of wearer; 1930-1935 at the very end of S.F.B.J. Company in Paris.
MARKS: "Bte.//S.F.B.J.//PARIS//9."

34

PUERTO RICO

Columbus landed in Puerto Rico in 1493, and because of its strategic location and resources it became a stronghold of the New World. In 1898 after the Spanish-American War, it became a possession of the United States. Today it is a very busy tourist and industrial island, offering "something for everyone".

35. Maid and Baby in Colonial Days: 7in (18cm); hard plastic dolls; maid dressed in dark blue dress, white apron, mob cap, pearl earrings; baby has a bottle molded in his hands; 1982.
MARKS: "Maid during the Spanish Colonial Times in Puerto Rico." tag on doll.
Thelma Purvis Collection.

35

36. Banana Cutter Man: 23in (58cm); carved wooden head; cloth body; multi-colored striped shirt; blue pants tied at ankle; leather shoes and belt with gold buckle; long hand carved, wooden knife to cut bananas; pants tied at ankles to keep out spiders; handwoven straw hat; 1930s.
MARKS: "Puerto Rico" on a paper pinned on doll.

36

37. Puerto Rican Girl with Basket and Guitar: 7in (18cm); hard plastic; open/shut eyes; jointed at shoulders; straw hat; red and black print dress; ruffle around bottom of dress; 1964. *Sherry Morgan Collection.*

37

38. *Left to Right:* **Dancing Girl with Gourds:** 6in (15cm); cloth over armature; red dress; straw hat; 1960s. **MARKS:** None.

Two Man Band: Two tiny wooden men; one playing guitar; second beating a drum; 1960s. **MARKS:** "PUERTO RICO" sign on stand.

38

ST. CROIX

St. Croix is the largest of the Virgin Islands. It was purchased by the United States from Denmark in 1917, and it still retains its Danish charm. On the island there are beaches, rain forests, botanical gardens, plantations, and, as on all the Virgin Islands, excellent shopping.

39. Topsy Turvy Upside Down Dolls: 11in (28cm); all cloth; two heads; clothing has two thicknesses; doll can be turned inside out, and it becomes another doll; one side is a red print; the other side is a purple and white print. Several of the Caribbean Islands make this type of doll.
MARKS: Made by the American West India Company in St. Croix. **39**

ST. KITTS AND NEVIS

St. Kitts (St. Christopher) and Nevis, both named by Columbus, are between the Leeward Islands and the Lesser Antilles in the Caribbean. They are a magic land of pink beaches and beautiful mountains.

They were settled in 1623 by Britain, who fought with the French for ownership until 1713, before winning by holding Brimstone Hill Fortress overlooking the route taken by the early pirates in the Caribbean. In the gift shop of the Fortress in 1995 was an unusual hand-made pirate doll. St. Kitts and Nevis became independent in 1983.

40. Brimstone Hill Fort Pirate: 20in (51cm); cloth except for wooden leg; navy blue suit with plaid trim; handmade; red felt hat; 1995.
MARKS: None.

40

ST. LUCIA

St. Lucia is a quiet, mountainous island in the Windward Mountain chain of the southern Caribbean. The terrain is rugged with beautiful beaches and rain forests. It has a "drive-in volcano".

41. *Left to Right:* **St. Lucia Grande Dame:** 11in (28cm); dark cloth; embroidered facial features; black wool hair; orange and maroon kerchief on head; red and white bandana print dress; lace trim; white skirt with lace trim; pink shawl.
MARKS: "St. Lucia" embroidered on skirt.

Nassau Child: Entire doll made of woven palm leaves; dress and hat decorated with raffia. (Nassau is the capital of The Bahamas.)
MARKS: "Nassau" sewn on skirt.

ST. MARTIN (ST. MAARTEN); TRINIDAD AND TOBAGO

An island divided into two parts, St. Maarten (Dutch) and St. Martin (French) is in the Leeward chain of Caribbean Islands. Only a sign on the road separates them. Eating food from around the world is more important to the natives and tourists than national ownership. Music is also important, as it is in all the islands of the Caribbean.

Christopher Columbus came to Trinidad just off the coast of Venezuela in 1498. Three sailors rowed ashore and climbed three mountains for a view. Thus, came the name Trinidad.

Today Trinidad is a busy commercial port which ships tropical fruits and vegetables to the world. Art and dolls are not as important. However, the lucky doll collector still can find a few dolls at the King's Wharf.

42

42. *Left to Right:* **Man with Red Drum from St. Maarten:** 8in (20cm); carved wooden head; wire body; blue straw hat; metal drum; 1995.
MARKS: "St. Maarten Netherlands Antilles."

Man with Striped Drum: 9.5in (24cm); molded clay; hand painted; orange hat; red belt; black and red striped stockings; multi-colored shirt; 1995.
MARKS: "Souvenir of Trinidad & Tobago Tourist Board//King's Wharf//Port of Spain, Trinidad."

UNITED STATES VIRGIN ISLANDS

There are 53 islands in the U.S. Virgin Islands. St. Thomas is the most populated and its major city Charlotte Amalie is the capital of the Territory. The scenic views, good weather, and wonderful shopping have made St. Thomas a popular destination.

43. Chiquita Doll: 8in (20cm); hard plastic body and head; rigid vinyl arms and legs; blue, green yellow plaid skirt edged in lace; white lace and net overskirt with hem-stitched trim; basket filled with vinyl fruit on head; gold earrings. Given to Pam by her grandmother in 1968. This is the way that Pam and Polly started collecting dolls.
MARKS: "Chiquita Doll//from the Virgin Islands."

43

44. St. John, Virgin Islands Family — Mother, Father, Boy, Girl: 5in (13cm) to 7in (18cm); All have cloth embroidered faces; parents have wooden chests, armature bodies; children have bamboo bodies, cloth faces; 1995. Father has a load of wood on his back. Mother has empty basket on her head; girl has multi-colored clothes and headdress; boy has white headpiece with school pouch on back.
MARKS: None.

44

CENTRAL AMERICA

The countries of Central America are Belize, Costa Rica, El Salvador, Guatemala, Honduras, Nicaragua and Panama. They form a land bridge between North and South America.

COSTA RICA

Costa Rica is the second smallest Central American country. It has a stable government which allows the people to live a relatively calm life. It is a highly educated country with a 93% literacy rate. The people dress in typical clothes of a tropical climate. Men wear colorful shirts and pants. The women wear light blouses and skirts.

45. Two Indian Women: Black leather hands and faces; armature bodies wrapped with yarn.
Left: Costa Rican woman wearing a multi-colored dress with a yellow apron.
Right: Costa Rican woman wearing a blue dress with a white apron. These dolls are well made with nice clothing; 1930s.
MARKS: None.
Thelma Purvis Collection.

45

46. Coffee Picker: 8.5in (22cm); stiffened paper doll; painted hair and facial features; mustache and beard; tan hat; white shirt; yellow pants; brown blanket over shoulder; red sash; blue scarf; paper sandals; carrying a basket of fresh coffee.
MARKS: "Hecho en Costa Rica for Buda Chavez" on base.
Sherry Morgan Collection.

46

EL SALVADOR

47. *Left to Right:* **Wood Peddler:** 9.5in (24cm); cloth; cardboard body; mask face; clay head; wool hair; papier-mâché hat; white cotton suit. **MARKS:** "Hand made in El Salvador" on bottom of base. *Beverley Findlay Collection.*

Ecuador Girl (from the country Ecuador)**:** 13in (33cm); hard plastic; brown skin tone; jointed at neck, shoulders, hips; yellow head scarf; gold earrings; red, white, blue beads; dark red dress; 1950s-1960s. **MARKS:** "AMA" marked on back; "Ecuador" on pin fastening dress. *Beverley Findlay Collection.*

47

48-49. Man with Votive Box: 12in (31cm); heavy flannel stuffed body; well-painted face; yellow cotton shirt; gray pants with red stripes; leather sandals; legs made to indicate he is lame and on his way to church to pray; 1930s. The man holds a small votive box with a figure of Christ with a tiny painted face, gold threads for a crown, red robe, little gold items around the box as his gifts to Christ when he gets to church. **MARKS:** "Made in El Salvador" typed on paper and pinned to back of shirt.

49

48

GUATEMALA

The Republic of Guatemala lies between Mexico and Honduras. Spanish is the national language; however, over 20 Mayan languages are still spoken.

For years making dolls has been a livelihood for many Guatemalan families. They dress the dolls according to traditions and legends of over 200 districts. A few doll makers, like Benjamin Garcia, are also interested in preserving the types of old cloth by making clothes for dolls.

The women wear corsets, long skirts with sashes and loose fitting blouses called huipils. Women from some villages such as Huetenango wear an apron or paya to cover their skirt. In the city their clothing is sometimes flowered or plaid. The men wear shirts and loose-hanging pants, often embroidered. Even today, cloth is hand-woven on home looms of simple sticks. (Dolls sometimes come with their own loom.)

Hand-loomed cloth is very narrow and cannot be cut. Therefore, styles do not change. One piece of clothing is the *tzute* which may form a turban, kerchief, sash, bag, or rebozo (shawl), which is the carry-all for everything including babies. Patterns may vary, but not basic clothing. Many people go barefoot, but some villagers make cheap sandals from old rubber tires and other material. In the hot region cotton is used, but in the mountains wool is more common. At least 5,000 fabric designs reflect 145 Maya groups. There are other concerns in the choice of cloth. Delicate patterns woven into the garments may indicate the wearer's social position, marital standing, number of children, how many sons are married, etc. In the holiday season, the women and girls wear the *cinta*, a headdress made of plain, rolled material topped with a woven band with Mayan designs. Often a long gauze scarf is carried for the festivities.

50

50. Guatemalan Peddlers: The people of Guatemala can still be seen carrying heavy loads on their backs. Many of their dolls are peddlers and the doll makers seem to enjoy making miniatures of their everyday loads.

<u>MARKS:</u> "Guatemala" on the bottom of their stands.

**51. Guatemalan Couple Coming Home
From Market:** Cloth over wire frame;
hand-loomed clothing.
Woman: 7.5in (18cm); hand-loomed blue,
red, white, yellow skirt; red, blue, yellow
plaid huipil (blouse); baby peeping out of
repoza (scarf) under firewood.
Man: 8in (20cm); yellow, blue, red shirt
with blue fringe; red sash; white pants,
straw hat with red decorations; carrying
firewood; 1960s.
MARKS: "Guatemala" on wooden stand.

51

52. *Left to Right:* **Woman
Carrying Vegetables on Head:**
5.5in (14cm); cloth head; wood-
en frame body; homespun blue
plaid skirt and multi-colored
blouse; 1945.
MARKS: "Kimport,
Independence, Mo.//This doll
was made in Guatemala."

Peddler Man: 11in (28cm);
cloth body, head; wood legs;
orange shirt; white, green, red
pants; red, white apron; 1945.
MARKS: "Handmade in
Guatemala" on bottom of stand.

Musician: 5.5in (14cm); cloth
head; wooden frame body; red,
white, blue shirt; white pants;
wooden stringed instrument;
1945.
MARKS: None. Missing
Kimport tag.

52

53. Woman Peddler: 9.5in (24cm); cloth covered wire armature; hand woven blue and green plaid skirt; multi-colored rebozo (shawl) carrying baby; basket on head; gem earrings.
MARKS: "Made in Guatemala: Totonicapan//District" on base.
Beverley Findlay Collection.

54. Guatemalan Musicians: 8in (20cm); wire-frame bodies wound with tape and covered with nylon; hand-loomed clothes with multi-colors; head covering is a reboza which also can be used as a carry-all (including babies); 1980.

The wooden marimba-like instrument is capable of a variety of sounds when played by a skilled player.

This set of dolls was originally imported by SERRV.
MARKS: None.

54

Many Guatemalan's are artistically inclined, and they enjoy handcrafts of many types. Their handcrafts include cloth pattern weaving, fringes, basketry, pottery and dolls. They even enjoy making what they call, "Possibly the Tiniest Dolls in the World." There are many variations of this theme.

55. Tiny Doll Family: Mother, father, and six children; 5/16in (1cm) to 1in (3cm) tall. Their clothing is made like the patterns of the colorful Guatemalan villages or sections. However, they do not use cloth. They wrap thread around the dolls in patterns so that it imitates cloth; 1950s-1960s. These are Kimport dolls. **MARKS:** None.

55

HONDURAS

For over half a century or more, the people of Honduras have been making colorful native handicrafts including dolls which are sold in local markets including the capital city of Tegucigalpa. Paper or cloth serve as the body of the dolls, and the clothes are made from pieces of bright, colorful scraps of material. The faces often are different from the dolls of other nations, but the stitching of the features give them a lively character.

56. Honduran Good Luck Girl: 7.5in (19cm); nylon-covered papier-mâché head and body; papier-mâché arms and legs; embroidered facial features; black floss wig; straw hat with multi-colored flowers; leather slippers; white, yellow, blue and pink dress with lace collar; white apron; 1960s. **MARKS:** "Honduras Good-luck" stamped on wooden base.

56

NICARAGUA

Nicaragua lies in the center of Central America. Managua is the capital. About 62% of the people are farmers and stock raisers. Nicaragua has less handcrafted dolls than most Central American countries.

57. Nela of Nicaragua: 11.5in (29cm); body made of burlap; body underclothes wrapped with Spanish language newspaper featuring Hot Point stove ads; embroidered face; blue print tunic with pleated ruffle collar; red and white plaid with ruffle at hem; glass beads; print shawl around her neck; 1944.

This was another doll imported by Kimport.
MARKS: "Kimport//Dolls//This Doll Made in Nicaragua."

57

PANAMA

The country of Panama is an east-west land bridge between North and South America, and the famous Panama Canal is located there. The building of the canal was a long, difficult process battling jungle terrain, disease, and disputes over ownership rights. Work on the canal started in 1904, and it opened to traffic August 15, 1914. The United States negotiated rights to run the canal, but by treaty these rights will end in 1999, and the running of the canal will be controlled by Panama.

Most Panamanians wear the same loose, light clothing worn in tropical countries. They do have a national costume used for feast days and special occasions. The women wear the *pollera* (see *Illustration 60*) and the men wear the *mootuno*, a white cotton costume which has a loose, long-sleeved embroidered shirt worn over fringed trousers.

The *pollera* has multi-ruffles with multi-colored floral designs. Gold and pearl hair ornaments are worn in the hair. Pearl earrings and necklaces complete the costumes.

58. Straw Doll: 10.5in (27cm); pink, purple, natural colored woven straw doll; facial features formed by stitching; doll is holding a straw bouquet; the doll was purchased in Panama in the 1960s by Pam's grandmother. This type of doll can be found in several of the other Central American countries. **MARKS:** None.

58

59. Man in Embroidered Suit: 8in (20cm); hard plastic A&H doll bought wholesale and dressed in Panama; unbleached muslin long shirt and short pants; hand embroidered with red thread; straw hat with red ribbons and wool pompons.

This costume was used for festivals and other celebrations.

MARKS: "A & H" on back of head.
Laura Brown Collection.

59

60

60. Doll Dressed in Pollera Costume: 9in (23cm); papier-mâché; purchased by the owner from Mary Lewis, first president of U.F.D.C., in the 1930s. The pollera is the national dress of the women of Panama. It is based on the colonial dress of the early colonial Spanish women. The dress has a deep waist, and a flaring high collar. It is made of white voile or organdy-type material; trimmed with yards of hand-embroidered trim and fine lace on both the bodice and skirt. The hair is sparkling with flowers, butterflies, flowers and pearls on springs. It is worn for festivals.
MARKS: None.
Lois Janner Collection.

42

NATIVE AMERICANS OF ALASKA

The people of the Arctic have been migrating hunters, fishermen, and herdsmen for many years in spite of the harsh, forbidding cold climate. Some of them still make their living this way. Others have adapted to modern living and even city life. In both living styles they made dolls. In the beginning they were hand carved of bone by the men. The women used fur to make the clothes. They made them for their children and for trading. Today doll artists still make dolls for the same purposes, but they use modern techniques.

HORN DOLL
by Vincent & Molly Tocktoo
Inupiat Eskimo

61

61. Horn Doll: 6in (15cm); body and head is carved caribou antler; the sleeves of the fur parka serve as the arms; the cloth hands are attached to the sleeves; fur covers the lower section of the doll; 1930s.

The dolls were often made by a husband who carved the doll, and his wife who sewed the clothing. They worked on the dolls during the long Arctic winter. Vincent Tocktoo, one of these dollmakers, became a spokesman for Eskimo Pies.

MARKS: "Horn doll//by Vincent and Molly Tocktoo//Inupiat Eskimo" on tag.

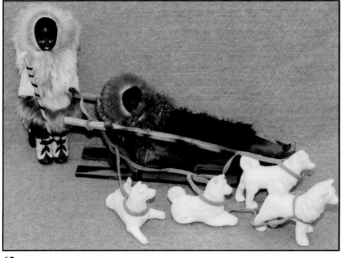

62

62. Native American (Alaskan) Couple with Baby and Dog Team:
Man: 9in (23cm); hard plastic; fur trimmed parka; leather boots; holding spear. **Mother Holding Baby in Sled:** 8in (20cm); hard plastic; fur parka under fur robe. **Baby:** 4in (10cm); vinyl; fur parka.
Dog Team: Made from chalk (plaster).
　　Purchased from a doll store in Fairbanks, Alaska, where it was on display; 1986.
MARKS: None.
Jean Horton Collection.

63

63. *Left to Right:* **Nuni Doll Holding Snowballs:** 4.5in (12cm); molded resin with wood chips; white fur parka; made by Bill Lee in Alaska after 1975.
MARKS: Same as *Illustration 70.*
Jean Horton Collection.

Doll with Carved Hair: 2.5in (6cm); Naber Doll; purchased in Alaska in 1986. (Possibly Silly Billy).
MARKS: "Naber Doll Company" tag on doll. *Jean Horton Collection.*

Sillikens (third from right and doll on right side): 2.5in (6cm); molded resin and wood chips; cord attached to heads. Less than 300 made.
MARKS: "The Alaskan Sillikens' on tags shown in picture.

Doll (fourth from left): 2.5in (6cm); two front teeth showing.
MARKS: None.
Jean Horton Collection.

Lady (standing in back row): 6.5in (17cm); leather face; sealskin parka; white boots; has toy seal in her hand.
MARKS: None.

64. Shot-Kee-Doh (Pretty Little Girl): 7in (18cm); felt head with embroidered features; felt feet and hands; reindeer fur body; date unknown.
MARKS: "ANAC//INDIAN//MADE IN ALASKA//CERTIFIED BY THE//ALASKA NATIVE ARTS & CRAFTS//CLEARING HOUSE//SHOT-KEE-DON (PRETTY LITTLE GIRL)//FLINGIL INDIAN DOLL" tag on doll.
Sold by Kimport.

64

65. Alaskan Native American: 12in (31cm); papier-mâché head; cloth body; three kinds of fur in costume; leather boots and mittens.

MARKS: None.
Jean Horton Collection.

65

66

66. Fairbanks Native American Couple: 10in (25cm); papier-mâché body; painted face; black yarn hair; felt winter clothes with orange artificial fur trim on hood, parka, sleeves; green yarn, hand-crocheted trim on boots, parka; green felt mittens; purchased in 1930s in Fairbanks, Alaska.
MARKS: None.
Sandy Strater Collection.

67. Alaskan Native Fisherman: 10in (25cm); steamed skin parka; molded painted face, shoulder plate, legs; no arms under fur parka; cloth body; striped cotton shirt; felt pants; handsewn leather mukluks (boots) and gloves; human hair wig; head and body stuffed with straw; carrying two painted cardboard fish; 1930s. Many of these dolls were made without arms because it was difficult to push the arms through the heavy fur. This doll is similar to the dolls made by Native Americans which were sent to Kimport for sale to their customers.
MARKS: None.

67

68. *Left to Right:* **Alaskan Tlingit Native American:** 12in (32cm); handcrafted; felt head; stuffed cloth body; embroidered facial features; ornate, bird-shaped felt headdress with iridescent beads in shape of bird; black wool braids; fringed brown dress with olive green beads; beaded blue felt cape tied with leather at neck, and decorated with beadwork frog; entire costume is ornate; imitation fur at ankles over leather pants; 1984.
MARKS: "Authentic native handcraft from Alaska" tag on cape.

South Dakota Oglala Sioux Eagle Dancer: 12.5in (33cm); carved wooden head with Eagle's beak on forehead; white fur wig over his own hair braided in back; cloth body over wire armature; feathered wood carved hands; imitation rectangular fur chest piece which extends around back; beaded disk necklace (imitates sun); back of extended arms have feathers to simulate an eagle; extended from leather belt are three fringed beaded pieces of leather; beaded shoes; in back at belt line are more feathers to simulate the tail of an eagle; 1981.
MARKS: "Doll Represents an Eagle Dancer Oglala Sioux. Maker Zelda Fasthorse" on stand.
Sherry Morgan Collection.

69. *Left to Right:* **Alaskan Native:** 9in (23cm); embroidered face; black fur hair; gray seal parka (outer coat) to keep out moisture, rabbit fur hood; black and red felt skirt; gray fur mukluks (boots).
MARKS: "Authentic Alaskan Native Craft//Made in Alaska//Department" on tag.

Nuni: 2.5in (5cm); molded resin figure; white fur coat; molded clothing.
See *Illustration 70* for additional information.

69

Smanisse Norwegian Native Doll: 7in (18cm); black and gray artificial fur costume is basically the same pattern as the Alaskan doll. Arctic natives roam free over the Arctic Region and have many of the same customs.
MARKS: "Arne Hasle 1800 Askim Norway."

70. *Left to Right:* **Nuni (Kiana) Doll:** 10in (25cm); doll molded in hand carved wooden mold filled with resin and wood chips mixture; beige real fur parka; black fur hem; carved black braids; doll beating drum; after 1975.

Harold Naber sold the Nuni company and trademark to former employee Bill Lee, who added "Kiana" to the trademark.
MARKS: A tag reading, "The Alaskan Eskimos have been making dolls for centuries. In the small village Mekoruk on Nunivak Island, in the Bering Sea, the Eskimos use rabbit skin to make their famous dolls. Our Nuni is a real collector's item. Each doll is handmade in Alaska. Only a limited quantity is available. By Kiana." The other side of tag reads, "Original//Nuni//dolls."

Original Naber Zipper Pullcord Doll: 3in (8cm); molded resin and wood chips; white fur parka; sold at the Anchorage airport gift shop as a zipper doll; yellow zipper pull cord is key to identification.

70

In 1970s airplanes flying from Japan to the United States had to land in Alaska and process passengers through customs. The Japanese aboard purchased most of the dolls. However, one American passenger, Pam Judd, bought a zipper doll for $4.95. Some Eskimos also purchased and wore them to zip up on their parkas. Mr. Naber has only one or two left and had not heard of any on the collectible doll market until contacted by the authors.
MARKS: "Nuni dolls//This original Nuni-Doll is hand-made in Alaska. Genuine furs are selected to fashion this doll//Anchorage, Alaska."

71. *Left to Right:* **Harold Naber Dolls:**
Upper Row.
Eric: 18in (46cm); wooden body; white parka with brown fur; black hair; retired after 1001 issued; 1991.
MARKS: None.

Natasha: 14in (36cm); wooden body; black pigtails; green eyes; white parka with brown fur; premier offering on Home Shopping Club; 1994.
MARKS: None.

Bottom Row:
Kilo (Baby): Puffed cheeks; wood grained face; eyes shut; black burlap hair; premier offering by Home Shopping Club; 1995.
MARKS: None.

71

Sissi Face Doll: 10in (25cm); head flat; soft cloth body; yellow parka with fur; lavender bow tie; brown, carved hair; bought in Alaska; 1986.
MARKS: None.
Jean Horton Collection.

72. *Left to Right:* **Northwest Territories Canadian Native:** 10in (25cm); hand-sewn, cloth body; black wool hair; heavy white cotton parka with hood; black cotton pants with trim; multi-colored sash; purchased in Montreal, 1974.
MARKS: None.

Alaskan Aleut Eskimo Woman: 12in (31cm); felt body; brown painted composition face; pug nose; black irisless eyes; orange mouth; fur around head; yellow and blue striped cotton dress; brown leather gloves with otter fur; fur boots; mid-1900s.
MARKS: None.

72

Alaskan Kuskokwim: 9.5in (24cm); hand carved wooden face; leather hands; real fur parka and hood trimmed with beads; seal skin mukluks and pants; 1984.
MARKS: "ANAC (Alaska Native Arts & Crafts) Lucy Hawk."
Sherry Morgan Collection.

These were never play dolls. At first they were used for trading. Now they are sold to tourists.

73. Old Man: 16in (41cm); soapstone; hand carved; wears white cotton summer outfit; sits on rafia mat; holds a short rafia tray; made to portray an old man left beside the way waiting for death; 1986 purchased in Alaska. He wears a man's rounded parka. The women wear a pointed one.
MARKS: None.
Jean Horton Collection.

CANADA

The Canadian people enjoy collecting dolls, making dolls and preserving their history through dolls. There have been many important Canadian doll companies, such as Reliable, Dominion, Commercial Toy, and others. There are also many Canadian doll artists who have created beautiful dolls. Canadians have always had an interest in their heritage, and some wonderful Native Canadian dolls, both old and new, are currently available from doll dealers. Canadian doll authors have helped collectors identify their dolls.

74

74. *Left to Right:* **Alberta Province Assiniboine Tribe Doll:** 13in (33cm); deerskin head, hands, feet; cloth body; beaded facial features; black thread hair braided with leader strips; leather head and neck bands; blue velvet jacket and pants trimmed with embroidered ribbon and sequins; leather belt; 1970.
MARKS: None.

Quebec Province Iroquois Tribe Doll in Crawling Position: 9.5in (24cm) by 4in (10cm); entire body made of strips of corn husks; carved wooden mask with fur trim; bead eyes; leather loincloth decorated with pink and black glass beads; pink and black wool strips around ankles; buckskin boots; 1978.
MARKS: None.

Alberta Stoney or Assiniboine Doll: 10in (25cm); wooden head and body; carved facial features; black wool hair and braids; beaded leather headband, shoes, belt; beaded white felt shirt and pants with fringes; made by Walter and Helen Chiniquay; 1989.
MARKS: None.

75

75. *Left to Right:* **Quebec Province Inuit Native Canadian on Ice Fishing for a Seal:** 4.5in (12cm); soapstone or steatite carving; hood with parka; excellent carving of facial features; 1989. **MARKS:** Tag that states, "Canada Eskimo Art//Hand Made by a Canada Esk. artist. Certified by the Gov't. Canada Artist Timothy Nayoumealuk, Inukjuak Community #66/5-26165. Date made 1983." The back of the tag is an Igloo sticker certifying the carving was handmade by the Inuit.

Province of Ontario Native Canadians: 2.75in (6cm); molded clay dolls; faces and hands are left unglazed; black glazed hair and base; glazed white dress stipled yellow and glazed maroon hood on woman; long stippled tan glazed parka with white fur on man; 1990s. **MARKS:** "KEENA." *Sherry Morgan Collection.*

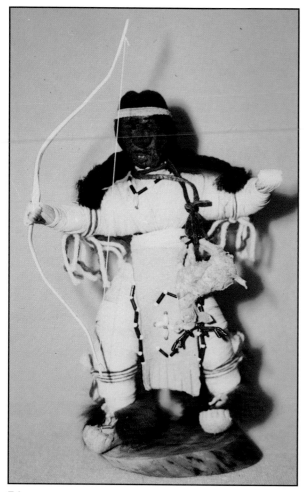

76. *Left to Right:* **Quebec Native Canadian:** 8.5in (22cm); dried apple head; cornhusk body; carrying a bow, arrow, and deer; leather, beaded Indian clothes; fur boots; Orieswekch, Ontario, Canada; 1981. **MARKS:** None. *Thelma Purvis Collection.*

76

77. *Left to Right:*
Canadian Native: 11in (28cm); cloth body; green Beacon Blanket costume; embroidered face; purchased in Toronto, Canada; 1990.
MARKS: none.

Bone Doll: 7in (18cm); carved from naturally shed reindeer horn; seal and reindeer fur; limited quantity.

Old Woman: Leather, needle molded face; cloth body; three shades of real brown fur; glass earrings; gray hair.
MARKS: None.
Jean Horton Collection.

77

78. Native Canadian: 14in (36cm); whalebone head is hand carved; fur costume; sealskin arms and legs; suede shoes; sitting on a platform made of ribs of whalebone; fish is carved from whalebone.
MARKS: Information on hang tag states, "Artisanata (Company). This carving is made by an Eskimo living in the Arctic and as such is guaranteed by the Federated Co-operatives of New Quebec which is officially recognized by the goverment of Canada and the government of Quebec. Artisan Pasha//Baron//George River; 1978."
Thelma Purvis Collection.

78

79. *Left to Right:* **Three Native Dolls from Canada: Girl in Fringed Skin Dress and Hair Band:** 8in (20cm); hard plastic; jointed shoulders; sleep eyes; black mohair wig; multi-colored beads decorating costume; papoose on back in yellow leather pouch; 1950s.
MARKS: None.

Native Canadian Girl in Dark Blue Skin Dress: 7in (18cm); hard vinyl body; jointed shoulders; painted eyes; leather cape; multicolored necklace; Indian drum attached to hand; papoose on back; 1960s.
MARKS: "Fait a La Main// Handcrafted in Canada" on tag.

79

Native Canadian in Pink Short Leather Fringed Dress: 8in (20cm); jointed shoulders; sleep eyes; matching fringed leggings; leather beaded headband; 1950s.
MARKS: "Made in Canada" on white tag with a picture of a bird.

80. Canadian Native Squaw: 18in (46cm); soft vinyl head; hard vinyl body; fully jointed; sleep eyes; synthetic hair in braids bound with leather, decorated with beige and white feathers and beads; genuine very soft deerskin dress and moccasins beautifully fringed and beaded; carries hard vinyl papoose on a backboard covered with a soft deerskin blanket; unusually nice commercial doll; 1960s. The bark canoe is handmade.
MARKS: "Reliable" on back.
Sandy Strater Collection.

80

81. *Left to Right:* **Huron Native Canadian Doll:** 4.25in (12cm), 5in (13cm); 3.75in (9cm); hand carved wood; beautifully painted; 1930s-1940s.

Man: Blue blanket with red and white trim; long hair hanging in pigtails.

Woman: Brown and black blouse; black skirt; white apron with red trim green scarf with white polka dots.

Woman: Rust blanket with black lines; carved pleats at bottom; red scarf with black polka dots; black skirt.

MARKS: "Huron//Indian//Canada."

The Huron Indians lived in the East of Canada around the Great Lakes.

81

82. Native Canadian: 12in (31cm); handcrafted Indian doll made of composition all in one piece with orange leather and suede clothing; trimmed with colored feathers.

MARKS: "Crafted in Canada by Indian art." 1970s.

Jean Francis Collection.

82

83. Native Canadian Boy: 13in (33cm); vinyl head; cloth body; rust-colored plush mittens; shoes; trim around hood and bottom of jacket; red yarn ties; clothes made of oilcloth; 1960-1970s.
MARKS: None.

83

84. *Left to Right:* **Native Canadian:** 13in (33cm); composition; painted face; human hair wig; dimple on chin; felt-like fabric dark blue top; red ties and shoulder decorations; red fringed pants; 1930s.

Native Canadian Doll: 13in (22cm); composition; molded hair; painted face; dimple on chin; chamois-colored leather dress; moccasins trimmed with beads; 1930s.
MARKS: "Reliable//Made in Canada" on both dolls.

84

85. Native Canadian Doll: 13in (33cm); Bisque head on composition body; brown and beige suede outfit; hair band with feathers in brunette hair; yoke, cuffs, pants are fringed; hair band and yoke are decorated with beads; 1920s.
MARKS: "P.R.P." (Paul Revers Pottery Company).
Jean Francis Collection.

85

86. Native Canadian Girl: Created by the late doll artist Dorothy Churchill and signed on the back of the head by maker; bisque head and hands; red native American costume; pointed hood trimmed with real fur; 1974.
Jean Francis Collection.

86

87. *Left to Right:* **Royal Canadian Mounted Police:** 8in (20cm); all-ceramic; painted face; red felt coat with gold stripes; black leather belt with pouch attached; black felt pants with yellow stripes; brown leather boots; felt Mountie hat. 1980s.

MARKS: From hang tag, "We certify the doll you bought is authentic, entirely designed and crafted in our workshop in St. Tite, Quebec, Canada. Historical themes, people, and customs of our country have inspired our artisans to create this valuable doll."

Royal Canadian Mounted Police: 17in (43cm); composition head, arms; cloth body, legs; red broadcloth coat with black leather belt and straps; dark blue cotton equestrian pants with yellow stripes; patent leather high-tie boots; police issue stiff brimmed hat; 1930s.

This doll is erroneously known as Nelson Eddy who played a Mountie in the movie *Rose Marie* in 1936.

MARKS: "Reliable of Canada" molded on back of the doll.

87

88. Anne of Green Gables: 8in (20cm); entire body made with a special type of plastic used by Peggy Nisbet; gray traveling dress with matching hat; painted gray stockings and black shoes; bright red hair with braids; multi-colored carpet bag for traveling; 1980-1990.

The setting of the famous stories of Anne of Green Gables was Prince Edward Island, a province of Canada.

MARKS: "A Peggy Nisbet Model//H200//Anne of Green Gables//Made in England" on tag.

88

89. Girl Guide (Girl Scout of Canada and England): 18in (46cm); felt face that is pressed until it is as smooth as composition; cloth body; blonde hair; deep blue eyes; wears a Girl Guide dark blue uniform; two patches on shoulder; leather belt; white shoes and socks. Doll was made in England by Dean's Ragbook Company; purchased in Canada.
MARKS: None.

89

90. Boy and Girl: 6.5in (17cm); cloth over armature; nicely painted face; girl and boy wear hand knitted outfits; girl is dressed in blue and white; boy is dressed in gray and rose; 1960s-1970s.
MARKS: None.

90

MEXICO

Mexico was the site of many advanced Indian civilizations. The Mayas, an agricultural people of the Yucatan, built immense stone pyramids and invented a calendar. The Toltecs were overcome by the Aztecs, who founded Tenochtitlán in 1325 AD. This is now the site of Mexico City, one of the largest metropolitan centers on earth. The Aztec empire was destroyed by the Spanish conquistadores, led by Hernán Cortés in 1519-1521. Three centuries of Spanish rule resulted in a multi-cultural society that incorporated many indigenous and Spanish traditions, creating a Mexican civilization.

The climate and topography of Mexico is also diverse. The dry central plateau reaches elevations of 8,000 feet and has temperate vegetation. The coastal lowlands are tropical. The northern portion of the country, which borders the United States, is a vast desert.

The sample of Mexican dolls, shown here reflects the wide range of types and prices. In general, the prices for Mexican dolls are low, but they are increasing.

91

91. Poblana of Puebla: 11in (28cm); composition head; cloth body; all original; dressed in red felt skirt with green trim; straw hat; carrying an axe. **MARKS:** None.

92. Man Playing Harp: 11in (28cm); composition head and hands; cloth body; and feet; wearing a white linen suit with a red felt tie; straw hat; woven leather sandals; exaggerated facial features; 1970s. There are many dolls of this type in Mexico; often they are holding a musical instrument. These dolls are reported to be made in Toluca, Mexico. **MARKS:** None.

92

93

93. China Girl: 16in (41cm); all-composition; long black braids; painted eyes; tiny waist; 1940s. This doll wears one of the costumes used for festive occasions in several parts of Mexico. It is called the China costume, and according to legend originated with a princess from China who was captured by pirates and sold into slavery somewhere on the west coast of Mexico. The white dress has a small waist with the skirt ballooning out over the hips. The green and red sashes add to this effect. The scene on her skirt pictures her capture. The doll and the dress are made of excellent materials. Another version of this dress is pictured in *Illustration 97*.
MARKS: None.

94. Charro (Gentleman Horseman): 16in (41cm); sculptured mask face; tiny rolls of fabric shaped into ears and sewn onto mask; well painted face with embroidered eyebrows and mustache; cloth body and limbs; black tight-fitting real leather vest and jacket which is hand embroidered; stiffened cloth hat with hand embroidery on brim; hand carved feet with low cut boots of real leather glued onto them.
MARKS: "Kimport//Dolls//Independence Mo. Made in Mexico."

94

95

95. Three Mexican Costumed Dolls: 8.5in (22cm); composition; painted faces; jointed at shoulders and hips; thread hair; 1930s-1940s.
MARKS: None.

Left to Right: **Girl with Red Print Headscarf and Bodice:** white belt; green pleated skirt decorated with multi-colored band; hem trimmed with red foil trim and white lace.

Boy with Decorated Charro Suit: mustache; paper-mâché sombrero.
Tehuacán Girl Wearing Variation of Huipil Costume: pleated headdress and lower skirt; red print band on skirt; white top with pink ribbons.

96. Dance of the Three Old Men: 7in (18cm); all three figures are hand-carved wood; painted faces; wooden flat hats; green checked shawls; red fastenings on shawls; colored ribbons attached to hats; 1980s. These dolls show a scene from the Mexican Folklorico Ballet of a dance of prehistoric origin.

MARKS: On the bottom of the stand it tells in Spanish that these musician are playing instruments they made themselves of cedar.

96

97

97. Bride and Groom Dressed in Michoacán Tradition: 10in (25cm); all-composition; painted faces; dark brown hair; 1930s-40s. The bride is dressed in the "China" costume (see *Illustration 93*); red velvet skirt with green taffeta band at waistline and bottom of skirt; white embroidered blouse; white spot on skirt is the only sequin left; holding wedding flowers in hands; sombrero is ornamented with a rose. The groom is wearing the "charro" or gentleman horseman's black silk faille embroidered habit. The real charro wears a suit of suede or velvet. The straw sombrero is embroidered around the edges. The picture in the background shows four musicians at an outdoor restaurant in Mexico.

98. *Right:* **Feather Dancer:** 12in (31cm); probably made in Mitia in the state of Oaxaca by the Zapotec Indians; headpiece made of short pieces of colored wool in a circle pattern; black wool body; white boots of homespun wool; yellow and red homespun short pants; scarf made of turquoise and back homespun; 1930s or earlier. (The doll on the left is an American-made "costume doll" dressed as a Latin American.)
MARKS: None.

98

99

99. *Left to Right:* **Mexican Corn Grinder Doll:** 6in (15cm); all cloth; embroidered face; pink dress with lace yoke; blue cotton print skirt with multi-colored flowers; holding a piece of rough wood which she rubs over an even larger, rougher piece of wood. The doll is balanced so she can reach all the way to the bottom of the board.
MARKS: None.

Charro (Gentleman Horseman): 7.5in (19cm); papier-mâché head and body; celluloid hands; black felt habit decorated with tiny pieces of gold glitter; black sombrero with "Mexico" written in gold glitter; multi-colored, hand loomed serape.
MARKS: "Hecho In Mexico" on base.

100.Pineapple Man and Woman: 11in (28cm); made of woven painted palm leaves; Lady has a green top; red and beige skirt; carries two woven pineapples with green leaves. Man has beige pants; maroon shirt; carrying two woven pineapples with green leaves. **MARKS:** None.

100

MEXICAN HOLIDAY, FESTIVAL AND RELIGIOUS DOLLS

Not only are there Mexican dolls dressed in costumes of various provinces, but there are also ones that represent state and religious holidays, both past and present. Many of these dolls represent pre-Spanish times. Some dolls are symbols of good luck and others reflect the music, dance and culture of various Mexican people.

101. *Left to Right:* **Santa Claus with Umbrella and Bell:** 6in (15cm); draped paper and cotton batting; small bell in left hand; 1991. **MARKS:** None.

Basket Scene of Children Breaking Piñata: 5.5in (14cm); woven wooden basket; grass and children of Sculpy-type material which has been painted and lacquered; 1991. **MARKS:** None.

101

102. *Left to Right:* **Donkey Piñata:** 10in (25cm); papier-mâché body; red eyes; green ears; yellow mouth; 1940. A piñata is used as a treat for Mexican children all year at parties or holiday celebrations. One child is blindfolded and tries to hit and break open the piñata with a stick. The small toys and candies stored in the fixture tumble out, and all the children scramble for their share. **MARKS:** None.

102

Feather Dancer: 12in (31cm); all-wool yarn; made by the Zapotec Indians in the state of Oaxaca. It represents the feathers of the plume dancers in the traditional feather dance for the warrior leader Moctezuma at the time Cortés conquered Mexico. This tradition honored the god Quetzalcoatl. Instead of feathers, the doll has crocheted yarn. (See also *Illustration 103.*) **MARKS:** None.

Pink and Green Strawman Made by Braiding Palm Leaves: 12in (31cm); wears a pink sombrero and green woven palm leaves. **MARKS:** None.

103

103. Feathered Aztec Dolls: 7in (18cm) each; composition heads; cloth bodies; feathered headdress over woven rafia circles on a stick inserted into a hole in the top of the doll's head; orange, and red cone hats; dressed in red, white, yellow, orange costumes; 1970s. **MARKS:** None.

104. Mexican Bullfighter: 6in (15cm); all-hard plastic; lavender "suit of lights" decorated with gold trim and sequins; red flannel cape with large collar; black felt bullfighter hat; 1960s.
MARKS: "Munecos//Carselle// Hecho in Mexico" on gold tag

104

105

105. Strawman: 15in (38cm); unpainted traditional Mexican doll.
The candleholder is an example of Mexican ceramic design. It is painted gray, dark pink and green; also made for years.
MARKS: None.

106. *Left to Right:* **Pottery Vase.**
Tehuacán Girl Wearing Native Costume:
5.5in (14cm); all-celluloid; jointed at shoulders only; black hair; painted face; dressed in all-lace costume; 1940s-1950s.
MARKS: "Hecho in Mexico" on bottom of stand.

Doll in China Costume: 7in (18cm); hard plastic; sleep eyes; jointed at head and shoulders; red and green print high skirt; white underskirt and blouse with red roses and green leaves; white Mexican hat with red raffia trim; 1950s.
MARKS: "Reproducciones de los Originales//Hecho a Mano; 'Myjy' Patent En Tramite//Hecho en Mexico."
See *Illustrations 93* and *97* for variations of the "China" costume.

106

AZTECS

Five hundred years ago present day Mexico City was the center of the Aztec empire. The Aztecs had built a large city on an island in the middle of a lake for protection. It was the size of some cities in Europe at the time. They developed methods of agriculture, manufacturing, and war techniques to capture other people because their Gods demanded human sacrifices. They also studied the stars, developed calendars, built temples, kept careful records, and created literature and art.

A major god in the Aztec religion was Quetzalcoatl. One legend wreathed him in plumes so the Aztecs dressed their warriors in brilliant feathers. (See *Illustration 103*).

Today, potters and carvers make modern versions of old statues found in archeological sites for Mexicans and tourists, and lady dolls are robed in Aztec-type clothes of the maguey plant or cotton (for royalty) with feather headdresses.

107. Aztec Lady: 14in (36cm); all vinyl; dressed in multi-colored print skirt and tunic tied with a belt; feathers in hair indicate her high social status. 1970s. Both women and men wore jewelry made from jade, emeralds, and opals. They also wore brilliant make-up — yellow and red for women; black, white and blue for men. The black ceramic vase and the wood carving also show the Aztec feathered headdresses.
MARKS on Doll: None.

107

108

108. Mexican Lady: 18in (46cm); composition shoulder head and arms; straw-filled body and legs; dark flesh color on painted face; dark eyelashes and eye shadow; open/closed mouth with painted tongue; red flannel skirt trimmed with sequins; white blouse with red braid; red cloth shoes with gold buckle; red, white, yellow ribbon in hair; earrings and beads; all-original; circa 1930s-1940s.
MARKS: "Ideal//Vida//Eterna" on tag shaped like a doll.

THE UNITED STATES

While the United States does not have national or provincial costumes, it does have costumes which relate to specific groups, past history, occupations, sports, holidays, Native Americans, and others. Dolls mirror the real world, and they wear many of these costumes.

In this section there is a special focus on a facet of doll collecting that has become popular recently: the Native Americans have been studying their roots, and they have been making costumed dolls. They are beginning to prefer the term Native Americans instead of "Indians" when they tag their dolls. The Eskimos are doing the same thing, and some of the dolls they are creating are in the Alaska and Canada chapters of this book.

HISTORICAL DOLL COLLECTING

Souvenir dolls have always been fun to collect, but there is now a trend toward accurate, well researched reproductions of historical people in the gift shops of many of the museums and points of interest around the United States. The prices range from inexpensive for common souvenirs to expensive for well made dolls done by noted doll artists. Institutions such as the United Nations and the Smithsonian, art museums, local attractions, and, doll museums are now places to find collectible dolls.

109. Margaret Blennerhasset: 8in (20cm); doll and clothes made of papier-mâché; red dress; gold necklace; cameo pin at neckline; black walking stick with a gold decoration at the top; 1945. The dress is a copy of a riding habit of 1804. The doll was made by doll artist Kathy Evans.

Margaret was the wife of Harman Blennerhasset, a wealthy Irish aristocrat. He left his castle in Ireland after he married his niece and fled to a wilderness island in the Ohio River, where he built a magnificent estate. Blennerhasset became entangled with Aaron Burr in the early 1800s in a plot to establish an empire to the west of what was then the United States. President Thomas Jefferson accused both men of plotting treason, and Blennerhasset was imprisoned. Eventually Aaron Burr was tried and acquitted, and Blennerhasset was released. Not only were the lives of both men ruined, but a fire consumed the Blennerhasset home in 1811. The couple and their children left the island. Recently, through a continuing program of careful historical and architectural research, the mansion on Blennerhasset Island has been recreated for visitors to see. The doll was purchased in the gift shop near the dock on the Ohio River where the paddle wheel boat picks up passengers to take them to the island.
MARKS: None.

109

70

110. *Left to Right:* **Early Football Player:** 13in (33cm); cotton cloth body; stockinette face, arms, lower legs, sweater; carrying felt football; blue cotton upper legs; gold shoes; early 1920s.
<u>MARKS</u>: None.

Early Football Player: 4.5in (12cm); all molded celluloid; gold helmet and socks; dark blue blouse; orange pants; black shoes; 1930s.
<u>MARKS</u>: "(Clover design)//Japan."

110

111

111. Nut-Head Doll: 5.5in (17cm); hickory nut head; clothespin body; red yarn hair; green plaid blouse; green pants and hat made from scraps of material; 1960s-1970s. A card that came with the doll states:

"This authentic toy gives you a glimpse of the days when your ancestors were building a great country without the aid of automation. All Blue Ridge Cottage Industries [products] are completely handcrafted out of native materials in the beautiful Blue Ridge Mountains.

"Hundreds of mountain families still spend their winters working on these sturdy toys while outside the snow piles deep in quiet cuts, runs, and ridges surrounding their simple homes. In the summer they work their small farms that their ancestors have lived and died on for hundreds of years.

"In their leisure they still gather to tell enchanting stories that nobody has ever written down. They sing songs that you will never hear played on your radio or stereo while they watch their children play with the same fascinating toys that thrilled their great-great-great grand parents (and yours too) long before the Civil War."
<u>MARKS</u>: None on doll.

71

112. Southern Gentlemen: 8.5in (22cm); sculpy-type head; cloth over armature body; leather hands and shoes; yellow vest; black and white pants; traditional white hat.
<u>MARKS</u>: None.

112

113

113. *Left to Right:* **Corn Husk Dolls:**

1. Lady with Red Hair Wearing an Apron and Scarf with Multicolored Stars: 5in (13cm).
2. Child Carrying Flowers: 3in (8cm).
3. Mother Holding the Hand of Her Child: 5in (13cm).
4. Child with Red Pigtails Holding Flowers: 3in (8cm).
5. Mother with Red Hair Holding a Baby in Her Arms: 6in (15cm).
6. Child Holding a Doll: 3in (8cm).
7. Woman Sitting on a Bench Spinning: 5in (13cm).
8. Young Lady Pushing a Doll in a Small Cart: 4.5in (12cm).
9. Child Dressed Up Like Mother Carrying a Broom: 3.5in (9cm).
10. Mother Sitting on a Bench Spanking Her Son: 5in (13cm).
11. Child on Top of a Slide: 1in (3cm).

<u>MARKS</u>: The dolls were made in different countries, including Czechoslovakia, Taiwan and the United States.

114. *Left to Right:* **Pioneer-type Dolls:** 7in (18cm); hand-carved head and body; unusual protruding chin; carrying a hand-carved wooden pail; black and white print blouse; blue check skirt and bonnet; lace sash around waist.
MARKS: None.

Cornhusk American Woman and Baby: 7in (18cm); well-made cornhusk doll; long straw dress with red straw blouse; red straw hat; carrying baby in her arms; purchased in Kentucky; 1960.
MARKS: None.

114

American Applehead Doll: 10in (25cm); carved, dried applehead face; wearing a yellow pioneer, or mountain, outfit and bonnet; 1975.
MARKS: "This is Genuine//Mountain handicraft//sold on Skyline Drive//Shenandoah National Park//Virginia." on paper tag.

Pioneer Corncob Mother and Baby: 7.5in (19cm); carved corncob face; rest of doll body is an ear of corn; blue checked dress and bonnet; lace sash; baby is 3.5in (8cm); carved corncob face; rest of doll body is a partial ear of corn; wrapped in flannel blanket; 1978.
MARKS: "Corncob/Doll//Dick Schnacke; Mountain Craft Shop//RT 1; Proctor, W.Va. 26055." on tag.

115. Selling Vegetables in Dixie: 9in (23cm); wooden head; cloth body over armature; black floss hair; head scarf made of white cotton with blue polka dots; yellow cotton shawl with lavender flowers and black dots; black blouse that is part of body; yellow dress with light red stars and black leaves; green and white checked apron, leather boots; hand woven basket with crepe paper vegetables; 1950s.
MARKS: None except tag seen in picture.

115

116

116. Casquette Girl: 9.5in (24cm); cloth body; elegant facial features; brownish-red long hair which curls slightly; lavender earrings; pink taffeta skirt; pumpkin-colored jumper top; white blouse trimmed with lace; red corduroy coat; 1980s. Information in a brochure attached to the doll tells that:

Weather, terrain and Indians were not as imposing a problem to Bienville, the first governor of French Louisiana, as was the lack of wives for his men. To solve this problem, Bienville repeatedly asked the king of France for prospective brides. In response, France sent 23 girls to the colony in 1703. They landed around Mobile, or Biloxi, as New Orleans was not yet founded. New Orleans received its first contingent of young French girls in 1721 aboard the vessel *Le Baleine*. Girls were sent to New Orleans from France intermittently from that time until 1750. The King of France gave later girls bound to New Orleans as brides, a small trunk (*casquette*) and a trousseau consisting of two dresses, two petticoats, six head dresses, and accessories.

These young girls volunteered to come to the New World and make homes in the wilderness. For the entire journey they were under the guardianship of the Ursuline Nuns. These courageous girls became the mothers of many families in Louisiana, Mississippi, and Alabama. Many Southerners today trace their ancestry to the "Casquette Girls."

117. Mardi Gras Clown: 9in (23cm); all-hard plastic; black mask; lavender and yellow taffeta clown suit trimmed with sequins; green net large "clown" collar; yellow net trim on cone-shaped clown hat; 1967.
MARKS: "Mardi Gras//New Orleans, La." on colorful pin.

117

118

118. Amish Dolls: The Amish people now live in many places in the Americas. Their original settlement in the United States was in Pennsylvania. They are still called "Pennsylvania Dutch" from an incorrect pronounciation of the German word "Deutch," which means "German".

Family Group dressed for gift shop purposes:

Father: 12in (31cm); "Baby Grumpy" doll; composition head and arms; cloth body; molded on shoes; brown wig and beard; 1936.
MARKS: "EFFANBEE//DOLLS//WALK//TALK//SLEEP" in oval.

Mother: 12in (31cm); different face; same body; 1936.
MARKS: "EFFANBEE//DOLLS//WALK//TALK//SLEEP" in oval.

Children: 9in (23cm); all-composition; mohair wigs; 1936.
MARKS: None.

The Amish do not make faces on dolls. At the right and left are Ester and Ethan, 7in (18cm) hand-made dolls that are constructed to sit on shelves with their feet hanging over. Ester is reading a book; Ethan is fishing. These two small dolls were purchased in Sugar Creek, Ohio, which has many Amish residents.
MARKS: None.

119. *Left to Right:* **Thanksgiving Dolls**

Pilgrim: 7.5in (19cm); hard plastic; sleep eyes; jointed at neck and shoulders; brown mohair wig; Pilgrim gray dress with white collar and apron; pointed Pilgrim hat; 1950s.
MARKS: None.

Indian Girl: 7in (18cm); vinyl face; hard plastic body; jointed at neck, shoulders, and hips; fleece Indian dress with fringe at waistline, arms, and hem; matching moccasins; colored beads at neck; glitter trim on arms; 1950s.
MARKS: None.

Girl in Center: 7in (18cm); all-vinyl; sleep, brown eyes; rooted hair; Pilgrim costume of black dress and hat; white trim on hat, collar, cuffs on sleeves; apron; 1960s.
MARKS: None.

Small Carved Wooden Pilgrim Pair: 2in (5cm); felt hats; painted bodies.
MARKS: None.

Carved Wooden Indian: 2in (5cm); tiny strip of felt for hair; painted clothing.
MARKS: None.

Pilgrim Man and Woman: 6in (15cm); styrofoam heads with netting over blue, brown, white felt clothes for lady; brown and white felt suit for man; white cap for lady; black hat for man; 1950s.
MARKS: "Shackman" on box.

Mohawk Boy with Pointed Haircut: 6in (15cm); hard plastic; sleep eyes; yellow fringed leather jacket; leather pants with fringe down the sides of pants; 1950s.
MARKS: "Deerfoot and Brown Eagle, an Indian family, are designers of American-made Indian Dolls; Carlson Manufacturing Co., Maple Lake, Minnesota." 1950s.

Pilgrim Lady: 4in (10cm); all-vinyl; white hat with orange hair, brown Pilgrim-style dress; white apron, collar, cuffs.
MARKS: "Russ."

120. Northern Civil War Soldier: 7.5in (19cm);
wax over papier-mâché head with molded green cap
and molded curls; painted blue eyes, blond
hair, rosebud mouth; wooden lower arms
with carved hands; cloth upper arms and
upper legs; painted ceramic lower legs; brown
with black trim to simulate boots; leather body with
squeaker bellows; green cotton tunic top and short
pants trimmed in red braid. The costume matches
those of the Civil War sharpshooters.
MARKS: None.

*Barbara Comienski Collection. Jim Comienski
Photographer.*

120

**121. Confederate
Soldier:** 9in (23cm);
vinyl, painted face;
inserted hair for mus-
tache; cloth body; red
hair wig; gray felt hat;
gray uniform; yellow
collar and stripes on
sleeve; black boots
and belt; carries sword
and Confederate flag.
MARKS: None.

121

122. *Left to Right:* **Civil War Soldiers:**
General Robert E. Lee: 8in (20cm); all-hard vinyl; sleep eyes; beige leather uniform and hat with yellow braid; buttons on uniform and collar; black boots; gold sword.
MARKS: None.

General Ulysses S. Grant: 8in (20cm); all-hard vinyl; sleep eyes; dark blue leather uniform and hat; tiny gold buttons on uniform; high boots; gold sword.
MARKS: None.

Soldier: 7in (18cm); all hard vinyl; sleep eyes; dark blue leather uniform; two natural-colored leather pouches in front and a larger one on his back; gold button on his cap.
MARKS: None.

122

123. Aviator: 16in (41cm); composition head, arms; cloth body, legs; painted eyes and hair; summer khaki aviator uniform, helmet; brown stockings and leather shoes; circa 1927.

The note pinned on his back says, "I am Lindbergh [sic], but I lost the Spirit of St. Louis. I came for Christmas, 1927 and have been played with by two generations. I was made by Uneeda."
MARKS: "UNEEDA" on back.

123

124. Marie Laveau, a Voodoo Practicioner from New Orleans: 16in (41cm); excellent quality vinyl; red kerchief and sash; dark blue skirt; white blouse; yellow scarf; petticoat and mid-thigh pants; gold earrings and bracelets; 1993. <u>MARKS:</u> "Gambia Doll//New Orleans, La." on tag.

Left: **Voodoo Doll:** 8in (20cm); red cloth folk doll with pins. <u>MARKS:</u> "Voodoo" on plastic packaging.

124

SKOOKUM INDIAN DOLLS

The following companies were involved in the sale of Skookum Indian dolls over the years: Tammen, H.H. Co., Arrow Novelties, and Geo. Borgfeldt & Co.

Mary McAboy started making Skookum dolls in 1913 in her home in Montana, where she lived among the Indians. She used a dried apple for the head. The dolls were so popular that she patented them in 1914. By this time the Tammen Company was making the dolls under her direction.

George Borgfeldt registered the trade name "Skookum" in 1915. He changed the head of the dolls to composition. The later dolls had plastic parts.

Some molded faces smile; others scowl; noses are different. Eyes usually look to the right to indicate good health and life; eyes turned left are rarer.

Some differences to look for in Skookum dolls are:
1. Eyes looking left.
2. Unusual, original wigs, especially gray.
3. Felt hats.
4. Very large and very small dolls.
5. Skookums wearing blanket with fringe.
6. Marked Skookums wearing Eskimo clothes.
7. Clothing made of buckskin.
8. Glass beads and beads with small claws.
9. Dolls with mailers.
10. World's Fair dolls with original pendant.

The dolls were made in a variety of heights from small baby sizes to 36 inches. Some of the large ones are now selling for $3,000-$5,000.

Dating a Skookum Doll by Its Feet:
1. 1913. Leather moccasins.
2. 1918. Suede put over wood; design painted on.
3. Early 1920s. Label on foot.
4. 1924. Molded composition feet.
5. 1930s. Shoes usually had designs painted on them
6. Late 1930s and early 1940s. Masking tape over wood.
7. 1950s. Plastic feet.

125

125. *Left to Right:* **Baby in Cradle:** 10in (24cm); black mohair wig; cloth body; bells to soothe baby as it swings on a tree; 1930s.
<u>MARKS</u>: None.

Squaw with Baby: 11in (28cm); composition eyes looking to left; face with sad look; multi-colored flannel blanket; black wool pigtails; real glass beads; wooden feet covered with suede; bead trim. The Baby is 4in (10cm); composition head; black thread hair; stick body; eyes facing right; 1920s.
<u>MARKS</u>: None.

Squaw: 11in (28cm); composition head; face has sad look; multi-colored blanket; black wool pig-tails; glass beads; wooden feet suede covered and design painted on them; headband decorated with beads; 1920s.
<u>MARKS</u>: "Skookum//Bully Good//Indian Character Doll" sticker on foot and on box.

80

126. Navaho Native American Dolls from Colorado: 10in (25cm); all-cloth; leather hands; both have a wool wig with a bun in back; 1971. *Doll on left:* velour top; plaid belt; white pants; red cloth shoes over cardboard. *Doll on right:* orange velour top; pink and white flowered belt; blue and white polka dot pleated skirt with orange designs. These dolls were handcrafted by Native Americans in Colorado. <u>MARKS</u>: None.

126

127

127. Left to Right: **Paiute Baby on Cradleboard from Burns, Oregon:** 17in (43cm); felt head; embroidered facial features; black hair; cream-colored jersey body; pink felt shirt; leather vest; cradleboard is made from a flat board that is edged with willow reed, and covered in hand-tanned leather; protective woven reed head piece; baby laced into cradle with strips of decorative leather beadwork; 1986. <u>MARKS</u>: "Maker Ramona Charles."

South Dakota Sioux Native American: 15in (38cm); dark brown leather head and beaded facial features; cloth body; buckskin (deer) ornately beaded Native American costume, headband, knife pouch; beaded leather moccasins; 1950s. <u>MARKS</u>: "Black Eagle" on tag. *Sherry Morgan Collection.*

128

128. In the early 19th century the United States continued to resettled that part of the Louisiana Purchase known as "Indian Territory," and later the state of Oklahoma, with Indians from the eastern forests. It was a hard, sad walk for the Indians, especially the elderly and children.

In 1889 the Oklahoma Land Rush occurred, in which American homesteaders gained land by rush and by lottery. Much of this displaced the Indians.

The black and white picture in *Illustration 129* was taken about 1904 by Seymour Wikle. His young son, Hugh Wikle, saw the agony on the faces of the Indians as he helped his family share their scarce water and food. He never forgot them. When he was in his seventies, Hugh carved the two small figures in the picture. He remembered the agony on the Indian faces he saw as a youngster, and that agony is on the faces of the tiny figures. Hugh Wikle was the father of Polly and the grandfather of Pam Judd. They recently noticed how much the sad face in the Indian picture resembles that on the doll and the two carved figures.

The doll on the left was purchased in 1994 by Polly. It was carved about 1950 by a Cherokee Indian who never walked "The Trail of Tears" but understood the agony of his tribesmen who had endured it.

The picture, the two statues, and the Indian doll serve as a tribute to the brave Indians of the forced march and the little Oklahoma boy who helped them and never forgot.
MARKS: None.

129

129. Kathleen Sioux Sitting on a Log in Lakota Tribe Attire Holding Her Traditional Buckskin Doll: 12in (31cm); all-porcelain; red, white and blue calico dress; protective beaded turtle amulet containing her umbilical cord and wild sage; muslin, beaded pioneer bonnet; beaded moccasins with mountain design representing the sacred land of the Sioux; limited edition of 1000.

The artist is Frank Standing High. He was raised by Indians on the Rosebud Reservation in South Dakota. He has a master's degree in fine arts and has spent many years teaching classes in Indian arts and crafts. His speciality is quill work, a difficult and time-consuming craft which has almost vanished except for the work of a few craftsman like Frank who are trying to bring back a lost art.

130. Native American Storyteller: 5in (13cm); baked clay; man with nine children in his lap. Made by southwestern artist Cleo Teissedre.

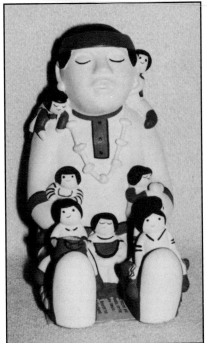

130

131

131. Native American Storyteller: 17.5in (45cm); molded clay head; two molded clay children listening to the storyteller; cloth bodies; tan, turquoise, and fuchsia wool handwoven costume; shell and bead necklace; white wool hair; 1991. Made by the Jennimarie Co., Colorado Springs, Colorado. *Thelma Purvis Collection.*

132

132. *Left to Right:* **North Americans**
Ten Seminoles from Florida: 5-20in (13-51cm)
cloth; a variety of dress colors; decorated with
braid and rickrack; made with layers of ruffled
material.
Three Small Wooden Kachinas: 3.5in (9cm);
painted multicolors.
One Large Kachina: 10in (25cm); black body;
blue facial lines; painted in multi-colored patterns.
Alaskan Aladeau: 11in (28cm); white fur trim.
Leather Native American Woman: 13in
(33cm); white fur costume and hood.
In Back, at Right:
Three Carved Wood Native Americans: 14.5in
(36cm); 16.5in (43cm); cloth body; red ties
around neck; white and red flowers on boots.
Penny Hadfield Collection.

133. Seminole Woman from Florida: Palmetto
doll; intricately sewn, quilted multi-colored dress;
small black hat; 1940s. Dolls were first made during the 1940s when tribal craftsmen founded the
first cooperative marketing enterprise for
Seminole crafts.
      This doll, which shows an ingenious use of
palmetto fibers in the styling of the doll, wears a
traditional tribal dress, that is quite different in
style from the later commercial dresses. Early in
the 20th century the Seminoles began using
sewing machines.
<u>**MARKS:**</u> None.
Lois Janner Collection.

133

134. North Carolina Cherokees:
7in (18cm); hard vinyl; sleep
eyes; jointed at shoulders and
head; heart-shaped wooden stand.
Left: **Squaw:** Rose print tunic;
dark rose leather pants and moccasins; rose headband; gray feather in band; 1995.
Right: **Squaw:** Red leather tunic
and pants; embroidered trim
down the front of the pants; red
hair band with
yellow ribbon; 1995.
These dolls were dressed by the
Cherokees of Qualla Reservation,
Cherokee, North Carolina.

134

135. Old Sioux Doll: 24in (61cm);
horse hair in strips for hair; fully beaded top; shell necklace and earrings;
buckskin trousers and long shirt with
fringe; no arms; legs sewn to bottom
of torso; beaded eyes and mouth;
stitched nose; 1900-1920, but possibly
as
early as 1880.
MARKS: None.
*Courtesy R. Murray, Trade Winds
Auction Gallery.*

135

136

136. St. Regis Corn Dancer: 10in (25cm); Kachina-type doll with mask; made from wood and corn stalks; leather apron-like costume with fringe at bottom; beads used for decoration; leather moccasins with dark leather ties; 1976. This doll was purchased at the long house in the Reservation in Hogansburg, New York. The reservation is on both sides of the U.S. — Canadian border.
MARKS: None.

137. *Left to Right:* **Hopi Kachinas:** Carved from one piece of light cottonwood wood; 1990s. Yellow Corn Maiden by Ted Frances, Jr.; Heotu by Sterling Francis; Kapon Longhair by Ted Frances, Jr. Hope Long Hair Maiden by Ted Frances; Corn Maiden Curl Mother by Sterling Francis; Hano Hano Mana by Sterling Francis.
MARKS: Name on bottom.
Buddy Wheet Collection.

137

138. *Left to Right:* **Kachina Dolls:** Hopi Mud Man; Hopi Buffalo Dancer; Hopi Eagle with Spread Wings; (Hopi) Black Bear (Large one in back); Owl Dancer; Hopi Falcon; Zuni Corn Dancer; Hopi Sun Dancer; Hopi Cloud and Hopi Hoop Dancer.

Kachina Dolls are very popular with men, women, and children. The ones made by Indians are usually signed by the artist. Some collectors enjoy a wide variety of tribal Kachinas. Other collectors prefer to select the Kachinas of a specific artist. There is a wide variety of prices. The most expensive Kachinas are the very old ones.
Beverly Findlay Collection.

138

139. Nez Perce Princess from Sandy Doll Co.: 11.5in (29cm); molded plastic; dark purple dress; fringed orange shawl; multicolored geometric design on bag; tribe from West Idaho, East Oregon, Washington State; 1994.
<u>**MARKS:**</u> None on Doll.
Beverly Findlay Collection.

139

87

140. Shoshoni Indian Dancer: 8in (20cm); cloth; beige felt clothes and hat; multi-colored beadwork; long black pigtails; beige moccasins with red and white beadwork; purchased from Kimport 6/6/1966. The Shoshoni tribe is from the California area.
Beverley Findlay Collection.

141. *Left to Right:* **Native Americans:**
Arctic: 10in (25cm); wearing brown fur clothes; gray hood. **Arctic:** 8in (20cm); wearing brown fur clothes; fish hanging down. **Canadian Yukon:** 8in (20cm); clay face; white fur clothes. **Arctic:** 10in (25cm); soft white leather clothes and body; carrying fish. **Canadian Arctic** (on sled)**:** 6in (15cm); fur clothes.
MARKS: "Mama 1906."
Cherokee Woman from Georgia: (See also *Illustration 128.*) **Group of Totem Poles from the Northwest:** Painted by Native Americans. **Papoose** (behind sled)**:** 6in (15cm). **Woman and Men Cheyenne from Colorado:** 5in (13cm) and 7in (18cm); dressed in white leather with beaded trim; 1940s. **Huron from Ontario:** 7in (18cm); all-carved wood. **Eagle Dancer from Kiowa Tribe:** White, beaded, handmade leather coat; pointed hat; 12in (31cm). *Penny Hadfield Collection.*

140

141

142. *Left to Right:* **Navaho Woman:** 14in (35cm); maroon, velvet dress trimmed with rickrack; beads around her neck; black hair. **Navaho Woman:** 11in (28cm); dark blue top of dress with light blue trim; flowers printed on

142

upper skirt;yellow ruffle around skirt; black hair. **Teepee with Symbol for Man:** 11in (28cm); leather; painted with Native American design. **Celluloid Native American:** 7in (18cm); celluloid; white top; black pants with white trim; black hair braids; wool hat. **MARKS:** "Made in Japan".
Stylized Cloth Native American Woman: 16in (41cm); cloth body; white wool dress with a high belt and flowered trim.
Penny Hadfield Collection.

143. *Left:* **Falling Snow:** 11.5in (29cm); cloth; from Nez Perce Nation, located in Idaho, Oregon, and Washington; white crepe collar; gray wool sash; red fringed skirt; brown leather boots; 1950 or before. **MARKS:** None.
Beverley Findlay Collection.

Right: **Sioux Burial Doll:** 12.5in (31cm); cloth; dressed in leather which was boiled in black walnuts to preserve it; robe fringed and beaded. The doll was placed with the dead to take away the evil spirits; 1950 or before. **MARKS:** None.
Beverley Findlay Collection.

143

144. *Left:* **Makah from Neah Bay, Washington:** 9in (23cm); hand-carved from red cedar; sweet grass hair; attached to red box which holds a pebble from area; heavy black eyebrows and eyes; red mouth; green; "v" painted on cheeks; back of head is flat; 1986.
MARKS: "Makah Cultural Museum" bottom of box.

Right: **Montana Blackfoot Indian:** 8in (20cm); carved wood face; black wool hair; headpiece made from black and white bristles and two feathers; cloth body; leather hands and feet; blue collar and loincloth; bells around shins; fake fur around ankles. He dances on wood base; 1986.
MARKS: "Thomas & Evelyn No Runners Browning, Montana."
Sherry Morgan Collection.

144

145. Washington State Makah Woman and Man: 16.5in (42cm), 13.5in (34cm); hand woven from sweet grass; black raffia braids and eyes; red raffia mouth; colored glass bead necklaces with olive shell pendants; early 1980s. **Man:** Body is woven sweetgrass; black and red striped loincloth. **Woman:** Body is sweet grass; dress finished off with red and black raffia in braided stripes.
MARKS: "Maker Vita Thom (85 year old woman)."
Sherry Morgan Collection.

145

146. Navaho Native American Loom Doll: Frame of loom, 7in (18cm) by 7in (18cm); wood; base covered with plaid material; all-cloth Indian woman with baby sleeping beside the working mother. The Navaho were herders of sheep which provided both food and wool to weave clothes for the cold winters. Like most Native Americans in the United States, they believed in the "spirits" and they could weave the symbols of their beliefs into the rugs and cloth they made. Gradually these people became famous for the quality and beautiful designs of their rugs and clothing. **MARKS:** None.

146

147. Skookum Apple Doll: 14in (36cm); molded composition head; cloth body; painted eyes; dressed in original brown felt jacket trimmed with rickrack; mid-1930s. The doll was an advertising premium from an apple company in Wenatchee, Washington. The company also offered apple labels and coloring books for children. **MARKS:** None.
Shirley Karaba Collection.

147

91

148. Many doll collectors have become interested in other Native American artifacts, replicas and historical dolls. The Mound Builders created an early culture. They left behind many artifacts in their mounds, which were generally used for burial ceremonies. Although the original artifacts are in museums, some people enjoy replicas and collect them as part of the early culture of North America. This pottery head is a copy of one excavated in the Seip grave mound built by the Hopewell Culture in southern Ohio; 3in (8cm); molded from clay; original of this head was found by H.C. Shebone of the Ohio Historical Society in 1927.

Other artifacts, such as pearls, tools, and ornaments of copper, silver, mica, and tortoise shell were found in mounds to comfort the dead. This grave probably held a member of the Hopewell people during the period 300 B.C. to A.D. 600.

The picture shows the Seip mound in Southern Ohio in the background. This is where the original head was found.
MARKS: None.

148

149. The Adena Pipe is from a mound of the Adena Culture. It is 8in (20cm) tall. The original yellow and red clay figure is in the Ohio Historical Society in Columbus, Ohio. The reproduction is shown in front of the Adena mound near Chillicothe, Ohio. The figure is similar to those carved by other people around the world.
MARKS: None.

149

KACHINA DOLLS

Kachina dolls are widely collected by both men and women. The old ones are expensive and much desired by advanced collectors. Because of the demand, more Native Americans are carving Kachinas. Those done by hand usually have the name of the maker on the base.

The Kachina dolls are a part of the religion of the Pueblo and other Native Americans of the southwest United States.

The Pueblo people are a series of tribes including the Hopi, Zuni, Navaho and others.

150. Eagle Kachina: 20in (51cm) wide wingspan; carved wood, painted and decorated. It is called the "Communicator" because it flies so high in the sky. **MARKS:** "EAGLE/./Julia Large Eagle" wood burned on stand.

150

151. Owl Kachina: 9in (23cm) tall; 4in (10cm) high; carved wood; fur added to head and legs; brown feathers represent ears; yellow and black bead eyes; light blue suede loincloth with deeper blue suede fringe trim. The Owl is the guard Kachina who keeps the "clowns" in line when they get too "wild" at ceremonies. The owl whips them with green sticks of the yucca plant. **MARKS:** "Owl//Wanda Ivan" wood burned on bottom of the stand.

151

SAND PAINTING

The Navajo have many healing ceremonies. These ceremonies last up to nine days, and chants are accompanied by dry sand painting made on the ground with colored grains of sand. These paintings are destroyed when the ceremonies are over. These paintings are also used in healing ceremonies by the Tohono O'odhum, Apache and Pueblo medicine people.

152

152. Navajo Sand Painter: 5in (13cm) high by 4in (10cm) wide; expressive face and hands of papier-mâché; arms and legs made from wound paper; base of yucca wood; Indian-style headband with red feather; red satin over-blouse; red, white, blue striped, slim pants; leather sandals with Navajo design on toes; multi-colored beads around neck, white and blue bracelet on each arm. The designs on the painting are wood burned into the base, and a type of colored sandstone is used to fill in the design. This doll came from a collection of older dolls dating from the 1900s until the 1950s. However, the owner believed this doll came from the late 19th century.
MARKS: "Navajo Sand Painter" wood burned into the base.

153. Indian Boy Key Chain: 2in (5cm); hard plastic; wearing a leather loincloth with a painted Indian sign; 1960s.
MARKS: "Greetings from Little America, Wyo" on mailing tag.

Souvenirs that could be mailed home to friends and family were very popular from the 1920s to 1960s. These tiny Indians still attached to their mailing card are now hard to find. The early ones were celluloid, which were fragile to send through the mail; however, an amazing number survived the journey without breaking. Hard plastic was much easier to send, but even so, some dolls were hurt or became separated from their mailing card. The date of the doll can be traced through the 3¢ Liberty Stamp on the tag.

153

SANDY DOLL COMPANY

154. *Left to Right:* **First Wind, Pawnee Woman, Ghost Dance:** 12in (31cm); maroon dress with silver stars; fringe on sides of skirt and around bottom of dress; long straight black hair; red, white, and blue beads around neck; brown felt hair band with one feather; 1994.

MARKS: The Ghost Dance began in approximately 1880 and was practiced by many different tribes.

"It was born out of the despair of early reservation life in the hopes that the dance would make the settlers disappear, the dead arise and the animals along with traditional Indian life would return to normal.

"This doll is clothed in the authentic traditional garment worn in the Ghost Dance Ceremony.

"The Pawnee have preserved many traditional songs and dances and continue to host the Oklahoma Pow Wow every summer in which many other tribes participate as part of preserving their tribal heritage." on colorful tag.

154

Apache Tribe White Eagle: 12in (31cm); painted body; decorated face; long black hair; highly decorated hat; warrior costume trimmed with fringe; carries decorated shield; beige protective loincloth; beige decorated moccasins; 1994.

MARKS: "Exclusively designed and created by Sandy Dolls, Inc. is the First Edition of our limited Edition Native American Dolls. Our limited Edition dolls come with their own signed and numbered tags and production is reserved to 5,000 to ensure the highest quality and create a collectible treasure." on tag.

155. *Left to Right:* **Sitting Doll:** 4.5in (12cm); multi-colored decorations on costume; 1977.

Wyoming Shoshone: Handmade dolls; leather over armature; black wool braids; nose shaped from leather; glass beads used for facial features; bottom of leather hands cut in strips for fingers.

155

Couple: (Man), 6in (17cm); dressed in white leather decorated with multi-colored beads; green leaf beadwork on loin cloth; real fur trim; circular feathers and beads on back; white fur and feathers headdress. (Woman): 6in (15cm); feather in hair; beaded white leather dress; matching beaded necklace, belt, moccasins; 1981.

MARKS: All have "Shoshone//Cecilia Ottogary" signature on base. She lives on the Shoshone Reservation in Wind River, Wyoming.

Sherry Morgan Collection.

95

156

156. Texas Native American Man and Wife:
Both 13in (33cm); heavy cotton body; and stiffened face mask; man has straw hair; woman has
grey thread hair; 1942. The man has a large
straw sombrero hat; red felt serape; black felt
pants with red patch; red cotton sash; red and
black poncho; white shirt; leather and black felt
shoes; carries a bundle of firewood and a stick.
The woman has a dark maroon, yellow, and blue
Indian striped skirt; pink and purple striped long
shawl over head and down to waist; pink under-
garment; leather and black felt shoes; she is also
carrying a bundle of sticks. A handwritten card
which comes with the dolls says, "Gift from
Mrs. Louis N. Beal, Kingsville, Texas. Home of
the famous King Ranch — largest in the world,
1,500,000 acres. The dolls were made by Native
Americans, on the Southwest border."
MARKS: None on doll.

157. Frontier Trapper: 10in (25cm);
hard plastic body; leather suit; animal
fur large hat; leather moccasins; carries
gun. This doll was purchased at
Disneyland.
MARKS: None.
Kathy Lincoln Collection.

157

158. Clapper Doll: 10in (25cm); all-wood; jointed at shoulders, hips, knees, feet; painted red suit with black trim; white shirt with tie; yellow wood imitation straw hat; long wire to control doll. This doll was found in the drawer of a chest in a house in "Pennsylvania Dutch" country. It was a popular toy and musical accompaniment to music at local gatherings, fairs and individual homes. The musician would hold the iron rod attached to the doll and make him seem to dance in time to music.
MARKS: None.

158

159. American Cowboy: 16in (41cm); all felt; painted face; black wig; brown hat; red scarf; red and blue plaid shirt; felt chaps; leather belt; blue pants; brown felt boots; 1970s.
MARKS: "KNICKER-BOCKER DOLLS//The L.L. Knickerbocker Company, Inc. Rancho Margarita, Ca."

159

160. Arkansas Traveler: 7in (18cm); papier-mâché head; wooden body; carries bundle on stick; dark blue pointed hat and pants; pink shirt; blue and white polka dot tie; 1970s.
MARKS: "Original Barnes-made doll/Arkansas Traveler; Ozark Shops//Native Craftwork//Ureka Springs//Arkansas" tag on bottom of feet.

160

161. Civil War-type Doll: 12in (31cm); made from a handkerchief; a knot is tied in one end for the head; two small knots are tied close to the large knot for the arms; lace trim used on the bottom edge. During the Civil War when supplies were scarce, women made dolls like this recent example from men's handkerchiefs. This doll was also called the Church Doll. Mothers could make this doll quickly to soothe a child in church.
MARKS: None.

161

162. Sugar Time Man: 8.5in (22cm); molded clay face; cloth over armature body; green hat and boots; wooden buckets and shoulder holder; wooden base; 1970s. In Vermont and in the Chardon, Ohio, area March signals the beginning of both work and holidays. It is time to tap the sugar maple trees, and boil down the sap to make maple syrup. It takes a winter of both thawing and freezing to make excellent syrup. **MARKS:** "Sugar Time" written on base.

162

163. Coast Guard Cadet: 7.5in (19cm); hard plastic body; blue leather jacket with gold buttons; white cap with blue peak; leather pants; 1970s. Made by Carlson Dolls. **MARKS:** "Coast Guard Cadet" on tag.

163

164. West Point Cadet: 11in (28cm); vinyl face; cloth over wire frame; cadet wearing the grey and white uniform of West Point, carrying a gun; 1965; purchased at the West Point Academy. **MARKS:** "WEST POINT" on button on his chest.

164

PACIFIC ISLANDS
FIJI

The South Pacific island, Fiji, became a British colony in 1874. In 1970 it became an independent parliamentary democracy. Fiji's main industries are sugar refining and tourism.

English doll makers such as Norah Wellings made dolls which were sold to the tourist's who came to the island by plane after World War II. The natives also keep their oral history alive through dolls made of tapa cloth which helps both the Fiji children and visitors understand their culture.

Many citizens of Fiji are Christians. This life-sized crèche in the central hall of a prominent hotel in Fiji welcomes travelers from around the world at Christmas time.

165

165-166. Tapa cloth dolls: 3in (8cm) and 5in (13cm); tapa cloth; wood fibers around head; 1991.

Stories and dolls have a tradition of being associated together all around the world. In Fiji some of the hotels have a storyteller and a dollmaker in a hut on the hotel grounds. The storytellers relate how the natives came to Fiji by canoe and how oral tradition preserves some of their history. A dollmaker creates a handmade doll while this tale is spun. (A storyteller and a dollmaker are in the background pictures.)
MARKS: None.

167. Fiji Policeman:
13.5in (34cm); non-flexible vinyl body; brown sleep eyes; jointed at neck, shoulders; hips; wearing English colonial uniform; blue shirt and white skirt; 1970s. This doll was purchased in Sura, the capital of Fiji. (The picture shows "The Dance of the Warriors.")
MARKS: "Fiji" on sleeve.

167

GUAM

Guam is the largest of the Marianna Islands discovered by Magellan in 1521. It is only 210 square miles. An important naval base, it was captured by Japan in 1941 and recaptured by the United States in 1944. Guam is still a U.S. Commonwealth and the site of an important American defense base.

168. Lady Doll: 10in (25cm); face carved from pogo wood which is native to Guam; no arms and legs; pink and turquoise cotton print dress from the Philippines; thread hair (the doll's original hair was made from a coconut husk;) 1970s.
MARKS: A tag tells that, "This doll was carefully researched by the Guam Rehabilitation and Workshop Center to find a product that did not reflect the influence of other cultures which touched Guam over several centuries. The stick doll is the only toy item found. The doll is identical to an actual doll of an 82 year old lady who said her grandfather had made it for her when she was a small girl. It and sea shells were her only toys."

168

HAWAII

Unlike the first Hawaiians, who arrived by canoe, the visitor to Hawaii, the 50th U.S. state, today comes by airplane or ship. The visitor is greeted by ladies in *muumuu*s who place *leis* around his or her neck.

169. Huapala Doll: 14in (36cm); dark brown yarn hair; painted face; cloth body; wears the traditional red flowered muumuu, paper leis around her neck, and a straw hat with flowers; 1997. **MARKS:** "V. Wong, Honolulu, Hawaii" on body seal.

169

170

170. Hawaiian Shimmy Doll: 5in (13cm);coiled spring between the legs and the body; painted fired clay; *lei* around neck; holds a ukulele; flower in hair; floss skirt; 1920s. When there is even a small air current, the doll sways gently. It was purchased in an antique store in Hawaii. In the background is an engraving of old Hilo, Hawaii.
MARKS: None.

171. Early Missionary, Mrs. Baldwin, a Doctor's Wife: 8in (20cm); papier-mâché head; spool body of crude wood; long pink dotted Swiss dress; mob cap trimmed with flowers; carrying a Bible in her arms; 1977. Dr. and Mrs. Baldwin landed in the Sandwich Islands (Hawaii) on March 31, 1820.
MARKS: None.
Laura May Brown Collection

171

TAPA CLOTH

Tapa cloth was made by soaking the bark of mulberry trees until soft. It was beaten into the shape of the garment desired. The *"pa'u,"* a long skirt made of tapa, was about one yard long and different widths. The women laid down and rolled into the dress. In the early days the women wore only a tapa skirt from the waist down. When forced by missionaries to change their costume, they added length, draped it around the top of the body and called it a *kikepa.* It was used in many of the islands of the Pacific.

172. Kechi-Iki (Tiny baby): 4in (10cm); vinyl body; dressed in *kikepa* tapa dress; 1972.
MARKS: None.
Laura Brown Collection.

172

173

173. Chief and Lady: Both 8in (20cm); handmade cloth doll; hand painted face, fingers drawn on hand; cuts in feet indicate toes; Chief is wearing a loincloth with a tapa pattern and a cape of yellow felt (instead of a cape of feathers). The Lady wears a *pa'u* made with cloth of a tapa pattern and a *kihei*, draped like a shawl and worn for protection against cold weather. Her yellow hairband imitates the feather *leis*. The *pa'u* consists of only a skirt and a cape. When the missionaries arrived, they insisted the women cover their entire body, and the *tapa kikepa* was invented. It is still worn by Hawaiian girls at festivals and pageants. The dolls were made by Thelma Gaylord of Honolulu about 1990.

<u>**MARKS:**</u> None.

Dee Percefull Collection.

174

174. Boy and Girl Flat Wooden Dolls in Wooden Basket: Boy 8in (20cm), Girl 7.5in (19cm), clothing can be attached to doll with velcro; 1994. The following information is taken from these toys:

Right to Left: **Kukane's Clothes:**

"Aloha! My name is Kukane which means manly. I live on the Big Island of Hawaii. My father is a great chief. I like to try on his feather cape and helmet. Sometimes I wear a gourd mask and pretend I'm a great warrior. I also dance the hula in my grass or tapa skirts, but my favorite is to fish in my canoe. I wear a cape of leaves to keep me dry."

"Aloha! My name is Nani meaning beautiful. I was born on the Big Island of Hawaii between Hilo Bay and the great Volcano, Kilauca. I like to play my ukulele and beat on my ipu. I love to dance the hula in my grass skirt and wear colorful leis."

Left to Right: **Nani's Clothes:** 1) Two piece hula costume with a white, multi-colored flower print; flowers on head, leis, and down front of grass skirt. 2) Pakemu'u, a short, modern version of multi-colored Hawaiian print. 3) Modern party dress with Christmas flowers. 4) The original muumuu with long pants the natives were forced to wear when missionaries came to Hawaii.
MARKS: "Dedicated to the beauty, peace and loving aloha spirits of the Hawaiian people and their islands which inspired this creation. Maryann Hibdon."

175. Hula Doll: 10in (25cm); body made from a base of sugar cane, coconut, parcellica (porcella); red cotton blouse; real raffia skirt; *lei' ai* headpiece; long white pants; carrying an *ipu*, made from a gourd.

When the missionaries came to Hawaii they were upset by the native costumes. They insisted the women cover their body when performing the traditional hula dance. Thereafter, they wore longer hula skirts, long sleeved blouses and long pants so their legs would be covered.
MARKS: "Makaleka, the island born designer, has created dolls long treasured by collectors. The elegant dress is handsewn and the fine Porcella face hand painted by skilled Hawaiian artists in Hawaii" on a tag on the doll.

175

176. Hawaiian Princess Doll from Big Island of Hawaii: 10in (25cm); porcella hands and head; cone-shaped papier-mâché body; wire arms; black mohair wig with bun in back; wearing the traditional formal red *holoku* of the island of Hawaii and red *lehua* blossoms in her hair.

176

The people of Hawaii enjoy their Island Princesses and celebrate yearly "their day" with parades, floats and beautiful Hawaiian girls. Each island has its own color, flower, and princess.

MARKS: "Makaleka, the island born designer, has created dolls long treasured by collectors. The elegant dress is handsewn and the fine Porcella face hand painted by skilled Hawaiian artists in Hawaii" on a tag on the doll.

177. Young Girl in Holom'u: 8in (20cm); hard plastic; jointed at head and shoulders; dressed in vivid pink, green, blue, white dress with ruffle around neck and hem; pink *lei* around neck; white flowers in long black hair; modern combination of the *holoku* and *muumuu*. The authors have noticed that Hawaiian dolls have been dressed in the islands by handicapped people for many years and that they are dressed with care.

MARKS: "All our grass skirts are made by the blind." stamped inside the box.

177

178. Tutu Muumuu Grandmother: 9in (23cm); round cork head with no painted facial features; cardboard body covered with cloth dyed to imitate tapa cloth (beaten water-soaked bark); white trim with attached pompons; woven straw hat with crepe paper *lei*; carries a wooden basket with tiny artificial food; 1970. This doll was made and purchased at a shelter for the handicapped on the island of Kauai. **MARKS:** None.

178

179. *Left to Right:* **Small Hula Dancer:** 8in (20cm); cloth with painted face; black yarn hair; grass skirt; crepe paper *lei* and wristbands. **MARKS:** "Waikiki" (printed in shape of mountain); made in Hawaii; copyright 1938, on paper tag on back.

Large Hula Dancer: all-cloth; painted face; black yarn hair; blue and white print bodice; natural fiber

179 grass skirt; red and yellow crepe paper *lei*; unknown date. **MARKS:** "Ka-Le; Hawaii" on paper tag in shape of pineapple.

Hawaiian Kisses: 8.5in (22cm); black with red flowers; green leaves; black yarn hair; 1980. Purchased in International Market Place, Honolulu. **MARKS:** Hawaiian KissesTM//I am the kiss of a Starry Hawaiian night//Honolulu, Hawaii." *Kathy Koliha Collection.*

180

180. Haleloke with Wardrobe in Trunk: 18in (46cm); hard plastic; blue eyes; eyelashes; open mouth with teeth; red felt tongue; black hair; walker; costumes include green print shorts and bra; natural fiber green grass skirt; neck and ankle leis; white fringed shawl; multicolored skirt and sarong top; 1954. (Haleloke was a television personality in the 1950s.)
MARKS: "Made in U.S.A." on back of doll. Made by Cast Distributing Corp, New York.
Kathy Koliha Collection.

181. Carved Wood Hawaiian Girl: 12in (31cm); jelutong wood head; cloth body; red flower print muumuu; yellow silk lei.
MARKS: "Beckett Originals" tag on dress.
Kathy Koliha Collection.

Hawaiian Children: 9in (23cm); molded vinyl; inserted black hair; yellow plastic flowers, green plastic hulu skirts; 1980s.

There are many dolls in Hawaii to bring home and love. This young boy and girl express the feelings of young visitors to this fabled island.
MARKS: Made in Hong Kong.
Kathy Koliha Collection.

See **Title Page** for photo.

181

182. *Left to Right:*
Dancer: 7in (18cm); molded plastic; mounted on spring; painted features; green skirt of embroidery floss; 1950s.
MARKS: "Made in Hong Kong" on base.

Hula Dancer: 5in (13cm); plastic; painted face; natural grass skirt and head-piece; real shell *lei*; 1950s.
MARKS: None.

182

Musical Shimmy Dancer: 12in (31cm); vinyl body; long black hair; green and white fabric bodice; white silk plastic *lei*; synthetic white grass skirt over plastic base containing music box; 1980s.
MARKS: None.

Shimmy Dancer: 6in (15cm); plastic body; painted features; synthetic grass skirt; spring mounted; 1950s.
MARKS: "ALOHA" on base.
Kathy Holiha Collection.

PALAU

The Republic of Palau, formerly a U.S. Territory, consists of more than 200 islands in the South Pacific.

In Palau, both Western dress and Philippine-type costumes are worn.

183. Lady: 10in (25cm); cloth over an armature body; molded and painted facial features; fine thread wig with a bun in the back; ankle-length, full-skirted dress with a boat neckline; a shorter skirt is draped over this.
MARKS: "BALINTAWAK//W//PALAU" painted on the base.

183

PAPUA NEW GUINEA

Papua New Guinea is the eastern half of the island of New Guinea. It is slightly larger than California. For at least 10,000 years successive waves of people entered this land from Asia through Indonesia. Europeans first visited New Guinea in the 15th century, but claims did not begin until the 19th century, when the Dutch took over the western half of the island. Eastern New Guinea was claimed by Britain in 1884 and transferred to Australia in 1905. Papua New Guinea became independent in 1975. The indigenous population of more than four million consists of a huge number of tribes, many living in almost complete isolation with mutually unintelligible languages.

184. **New Guinea Lady:** 7in (18cm); vinyl head with rooted hair; hard plastic body; skirt made of banana leaves sewn together; handmade beaded necklaces; baby is carried in woven basket; 1966. The owner visited Papua New Guinea, and met a missionary who later sent her this doll, which was dressed by the natives. **MARKS:** None.
Thelma Purvis Collection.

184

185. *Left to Right:* **Suspension Hook in the Sepik Style Form of a Human Figure:** 21in (53cm); elongated figure which the tribes considered an ancestor figure. The hands at the side are holding carved crocodiles and hooks which are used to bring home the "kill". 1950s. This is a way to give thanks to their forefathers for their knowledge and cultural heritage. The carving shoes the elongated skulls and beaky nose of the natives. In the region of Sepik, a few of the boys are apprenticed to woodworkers. New Guinea was one of the last countries in the world where cannibalism was practiced. **MARKS:** None.

New Guinea Wolf Ceremonial Flute: Carved wood with cowrie shell eyes; figure on top is removed to play the flute. **MARKS:** None.

185

PHILLIPPINES

There are some 7,100 islands in the Republic of the Philippines. A large percentage of the population lives on the eleven largest islands. The archipelago was visited by Magellan in 1521. Spain ceded the islands to the United States in 1898, following the Spanish-American War. Independence was proclaimed on July 4, 1946.

The clothing of the people reflects the different ethnic groups of the Philippines. The largest is Malayan, others include Negrito, Muslim (Moros), and Ingerots.

186

186. *Front:* **Dancing the Tinikling:** Set of four 6in (15cm) dolls; sculptured clay heads; cloth bodies on armature; men wear blue and red cotton pants with contrasting cotton shirts worn outside the trousers; women wear a dress with "butterfly" sleeves; 1950. (The *Tinikling* is a dance similar to jump rope.)
MARKS: None.

Bride: 9.5in (24cm); cloth over armature; needle sculpture facial features; black wig; pearl earrings; off-shoulder bridal gown with butterfly sleeves; 1970s.
MARKS: None.

187. Moros Couple: 9in (23cm); cloth over armature; painted face; man wears white shirt with yellow band down the front; rose-colored short coat with pearl buttons; yellow jodphur-type pants with green embroidery; scarf around head knotted at the side; carries a knife in a wide pink band at the waist. Woman wears a matching Muslim costume with hip-length rose satin jacket; silver necklace with a pearl; yellow satin pants; 1980s.
MARKS: Kimport Dolls.

187

188. Six Philippine Dolls: 5in (13cm); papier-mâché heads; cloth over armature bodies; **188**
1960s.
Left to Right: 1) **Lady:** Orange plaid dress with butterfly sleeves and embroidery. 2) **Peddler:**
Long green and white print shirt; long pants. 3) **Man Pounding Grains:** Red pants; maroon
and black long shirt. 4) **Peddler Woman:** Plaid costume with wide arched sleeves of rengue
cloth. 5) **Peddler Man Selling Meals:** White shirt and red pants. 6) **Lady Shopper:** Green,
white, pink dress with butterfly sleeves; ornate straw hat; bananas and other fruit in basket;
fish in left hand.
<u>MARKS</u>: None.

189. Lady of Ilocano tribe: 11in (28cm); painted face; yarn
hair; cloth over armature body; wears hand-woven wrap-
around skirt; bead necklace; 1940.
<u>MARKS</u>: None.
Betsy Toft Collection.

189

113

190. Negrito Man: 11in (28cm) all-cloth body; painted facial features; dressed in a loincloth with a knife in his belt; he carries a long arrow but is missing his bow.
MARKS: None.

190

PITCAIRN ISLAND

Pitcairn is a remote island in the South Pacific. It was settled by mutineers of the HMS Bounty in 1790. Still a British colony, the island is only 1.7 square miles in area and has a population of less than 60 persons.
MARKS: None.

191. Pitcairn Island Man: 10.5in (27cm); carved balsa wood; face drawn with a pen; jointed head and arms; legs carved separately; blue cotton pants and white shirt. (When the authors ordered this doll from Kimport, they had to wait six months for delivery because of the infrequency of shipments from Pitcairn Island.)
MARKS: None.

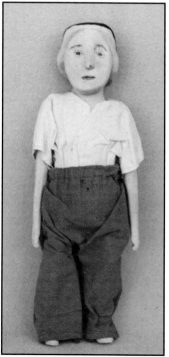

191

AMERICAN SAMOA

American Samoa is the most southerly of all lands under U.S. sovereignty. It is an unincorporated territory of seven small islands of the eastern Samoan group. The capital is Pago Pago. The American Samoans are of Polynesian origin.

192. Hula Dancer from Pogo Pogo: 9in (23cm); cloth body; dress of tapa cloth and straw. (For more information about tapa cloth see page 104.)
MARKS: "Pogo Pogo" printed on the edge of the skirt.

192

TAHITI

Tahiti is one of the best known of the some 130 islands of French Polynesia. While the major city, Papeete, is now a modern resort, most of the islands still are unspoiled tropical paradises.

193. Dancing Girl: 10.5in (27cm); soft vinyl; painted features; long black cotton hair glued on; straw crown-shaped hat and straw skirt; jointed arms; yellow snail necklace; imitation tapa halter; 1978.
MARKS: None.
Sherry Morgan Collection.

193

115

ARGENTINA

Immigrants from many lands were attracted to Argentina because of its agricultural and industrial potential.

The ornate gaucho costumes of the men are interesting. Gauchos are the "cowboys" of the Pampas (the plains). The lady doll costumes are similar to the pioneer costumes of other plains countries, including the United States. For the most part the full skirts are ankle length cotton or calico with beautiful trims, especially around the hemline. Traditionally, an apron was worn for work, and a shawl was used for warmth. The Indians of Argentina weave their cloth in bright colors and wear silver jewelry as they do in many other South American nations.

194

194. Gaucho and Lady. Gaucho: 13.5in (34cm); vinyl; white shirt; black bolero-type jacket with red cuffs; trim down the front of jacket; *bombachas* (baggy cotton white and blue check trousers) are tucked into boots when riding on Pampas; *rasta* (belt with silver decorations). Bola balls hang from the waist and are used like a lariat. **Lady:** 12.5in (32cm); vinyl; braided hair; white cotton blouse with blue trim on sleeves; wide gathered skirt with multi-colored trim on wide waistband and at bottom; red felt hat with brim which is held on head with sheer white scarf that is usually worn by married women. Circa 1970s.

MARKS: None.

Shirley Karaba Collection.

116

195. Argentinian Cowboy: 14in (36cm); cloth; felt mask face and hands; black leather legs imitating boots; black wool baggy pants; blue and white plaid shirt; white neckerchief; yellow serape; black felt hat and bolero; tied under his chin; brow band (*vincha*) to keep hair out of eyes; wooden bolo balls; patent leather belt with gold ball trim; 1920s-1930s. **MARKS:** None.

Small Boy Cowboy: 3in (8cm); wears a similar outfit. **MARKS:** None; 1930s.

195

196. Gaucho: 19in (48cm); cloth "smoker" doll with "lighted" cigarette; mask face; "5 o'clock shadow" on face; painted hair on arm; black wool mustache and hair; red wool poncho over shoulders; blue and white checked shirt; black felt *chiripa* (wide gaucho pants) over white *bombachas* (breeches) tucked in white leather boots with metal spurs; leather belt (*rasta*) fastened with silver chains; knife tucked in belt; *vincha* (white brow band) under black felt gaucho hat; black felt kerchief around neck; 1920s-1930s. The illusion of a lighted cigarette is created with red tinfoil. The cigarette actually looks lighted in a dark room. **MARKS:** None.

196

197. Indian: 19in (48cm); reddish felt body; red, white and pink felt Indian clothes; headpiece of feathers; unknown maker; 1920s-1930s.
MARKS: When purchased by the owner it had a hand written note saying it was from Argentine. *Shirley Karaba Collection.*

197

198. Gaucho: 10in (25cm); vinyl; painted face; black mustache; authentically dressed in black-checked, baggy pants; high white collar; high black boots; short jacket; white shirt; colorful serape over shoulder; black felt hat with small brim tied under his chin; brow band (vincha) keeps his hair out of his eyes; black sombrero; 1960s.
MARKS: None.

198

Lencilandia Girl Carrying a Bunch of Peaches: 12in (31cm); brown bun on top of head; red felt scarf; white collar; red blouse; green overblouse; red, blue and green felt skirt with white flower trim; 1920s-1930s.
MARKS: "Lencilandia" on inside of clothes.

199

200

The Lencilandia Doll Company of Argentina made felt dolls similar to Lenci dolls of Italy. They are not easy to find, but they are exciting to see in a collection. They are priced considerably less than Lenci dolls. The 100% wool felt Lencilandia dolls have a pocket in back for storing handkerchiefs, nightwear, etc.

200. Lencilandia Boudoir-type Dolls: *Left to Right:* **Blonde Lady:** Apron-type red dress, white blouse and white skirt have multi-colored embroidery; red hat with embroidery and yellow feathers. **Brunette Lady:** White sickle in hand; white, red, green and orange multi-colored dress; orange scarf. **Lady with Bananas:** Tall yellow hat, red bolero with white trim; white blouse; multicolored blue, red, green and white striped skirt; hem trimmed with felt flowers; carrying yellow bananas; 1920s-1930s.
MARKS: "Lencilandia" on paper tag.

119

BOLIVIA

Most of Bolivia is in the central Andes Mountains. The majority of the population lives in the Altiplano, the central plateau of 12,000 feet, with few resources. Lake Titicaca on the border of Peru is the highest navigable lake in the world (12,506 feet). Most of the people are of Indian descent but the culture is also influenced by three centuries of Spanish domination, which ended in 1825.

201. Witch Doctor Market: There is a large market in downtown La Paz, the administrative capital of Bolivia. Many women, who are called witch doctors, have small booths and sell food, pottery and charms. Bolivians buy these charms to help them through a family crisis. Since having a large family is important in the Bolivian culture, fertility symbols are important.

The women sell doll forms made of

201 cloth, wood, stone, etc. with a box of charms which must be displayed prominently in the home at all times and looked at each day. The charms are little tin figures, raffia, dried berries, and pieces of paper.

Polly Judd bought the charm in the right hand corner, in front of the photograph taken at the market. The Witch Doctor's bowler hat is an example of the hats often found on Bolivian dolls.

202. Bolivian Peddler Doll: 4.5in (12cm); molded, painted clay; hand knitted Bolivian hat with ear flaps for the cold mountain climate. This is a modern peddler and he carries leather sandals, a toy racing car, a clay pot, a woven basket, corn and other grain, and toy money.

The peddler doll is part of the Indian witchcraft ritual. When a family buys or builds a new home, they purchase a peddler with a loaded pack. These dolls can be from 3 inches (8cm) to 3 feet (91cm). Each January tradition says that there must be an addition to the pack to insure a bountiful year. **MARKS:** None.

202

203. The Dolls of Lake Titicaca: 5in (13cm); yarn wrapped around wire body; cloth head with embroidered features; lady is dressed in a yellow llama wool dress; maroon embroidered llama wool cape; green yarn hat and leggings; the boy has a shirt of hand woven llama wool; red llama wool pants wound around wire legs; wool crocheted blue and white hat; carries a flute; 1980. (Lake Titicaca is in the photograph in the background.)
MARKS: None.

203

204. Bolivian Wall Hanging: This type of chain-stitched, hand-woven wall hanging is made in a tiny Peruvian town of Chijnaya by children. This craftwork was taught to them by Peace Corps volunteers. The children make their own designs, and finished products are sold to tourists; 1980. This wall hanging shows the costumes of Bolivian Indians. The doll is described in *Illustration 208.*

204

205. Boy Playing Flute: 9in (23cm); composition head; cloth body; painted face; knitted hand-woven hat with red and blue trim; multi-colored threads at top of hat; red hand-woven sweater with yellow trim; black knee pants; 1970s.
MARKS: None.

205

BOLIVIANS

206. Man Playing Flute: 9in (23cm); cloth; multi-colored serape; black wool short pants with white and yellow trim around bottom; carrying flute; 1980s.
Lady and Baby: 11in (28cm); cloth; stiff bowler hat made from llama wool; green wool sweater; multi-colored serape and skirt; a baby peeks out from serape, 1980s.
MARKS: None.

206

207. *Left:* **Bolivian Dancer:** 12in (31cm); cloth head; embroidered features; real hair wig; armature body wrapped with pink and white thin wool yarn; stiff green bowler-type hat with pink sequins; handwoven strips across shoulders; hand-woven cloth used for pants decorated with green and pink sequins; 1980. He is doing a rope twirling dance to entertain visitors.

Sucre Man: Sucre is the judicial capital of Bolivia; 12in (31cm); leather helmet is family heirloom; carries a red wooden staff, a sign of his position. (Bolivia has two capital cities.) The wall in the background photograph is from the pre-Spanish city Tiahuanacu.

<u>MARKS</u>: None.

208. Masked Devil Dancers: 6in (15cm); molded, painted clay and cloth; white dancing suits; red and blue capes trimmed with sequins, gold braid, embroidery, fringe; clay mask painted bright colors. (These are from Indian legends of demons.)

<u>MARKS</u>: None.

BRAZIL

Pedro Alvares Cabral, a Portuguese navigator, is credited as the first European to reach Brazil, in 1500. Independence from Portugal was proclaimed in 1822.

209

209. Girl with Guitar: 22in (56cm); all-cloth; painted face; orange dress with black felt trim; 1920s-1930s.
MARKS: "Fabrica de bonecas 'Marpols'//Holzer & Cie—S. Paulo" on tag on dress.
Mary Merritt Collection.

210. Theatre Carnival Dancer: 16in (41cm); molded hard rubber; blue dress covered with sequins and blue boa feathers; 1980s.
MARKS: None.

210

211. Carnival Doll: 12in (31cm); base dress covered with white and red sequins, boa feathers headdress; 1980s. (These dolls can be found in the shops that sell Carnival, or Mardi Gras, costumes year around.)
MARKS: None.

211

JOAO PEROTTI DOLLS
BRAZIL

During the late 1920s and early 1930s Perotti made high quality felt dolls in Brazil. These are art dolls and resemble Lenci dolls, except for the color of their skin. The quality of the costumes is excellent. Joao Perotti was one of the first South American doll makers to be accepted by Kimport, a doll mail order company in the United States. The first doll exported was *Rosa*, a little girl with a big basket of fruit on her head.

Common Characteristics of Perotti Dolls:
1. Dark felt face mask; dark felt body.
2. Long black eyebrows; eyelashes on sides of eyes; small mouth.
3. Colorful felt clothes with felt decorations.
4. **MARKS:** "Manufactura Orbis//Joao Perotti-S.Paulo//Industria Brazileira" printed on small seal somewhere on doll.

212. Fruit Peddler: 14.5in (37cm); dark felt body; woven basket with felt fruit; orange and blue costume trimmed with rickrack; white apron with lace; 1960s-1970s.
MARKS: "Perotti" on tag inside dress.
Shirley Karaba Collection.

212

213. Brazilian Girl: 10in (25cm); felt; woven basket on head with felt vegetables and flowers; red dress with blue felt trim; red dotted swiss apron with lace; green and red shoes; black wig; 1930s. **Brazilian Boy:** 9in (23cm); felt; green hat; red scarf; blue and red plaid shirt; red pants with glued patch on knee; 1930s. These are Kimport dolls. **MARKS:** "Holzer & Cie" on tag.

213

214. Girl Carrying a Basket of Vegetables: 12in (31cm); light brown felt face, legs, arms, cloth body; hand-painted face; black eyes with white dot and half moon-shaped highlights in eye; eyelashes above eyes; heart-shaped lips; arm joints operate jointly; no ears; pink felt skirt with blue felt picot trim, flowers and black felt leaves; blue felt scarf with pink felt picot trim and flowers; pink organdy blouse with pleated cuffs trimmed with lace; blue felt clogs with white picot trim and wooden soles; black mohair wig;large metal earrings; circa 1920-1930. **MARKS:** "Fabrica de bonecas 'Marpols'//Holzer & Cie -S. Paulo" on paper tag glued to doll's teddy.

214

127

215. *Left to Right:* **Brazilian Peddler:** 11in (28cm); royal blue suit with wide pants; large Mexican hat; red tie and sash; decorated with multicolored felt flowers; wooden yoke for carrying baskets; 1925-1935.
MARKS: See page 126.

Doll with Guitar: 9in (23cm) decorated wood guitar; sits in sewing basket which still has old needles, pins, thread, button hook, and tape measure; orange dress with black trim; black velvet hat with orange trim.
MARKS: See page 126.

Little Girl: 9in (23cm); black thread hair with two tightly braided buns at each side of face; wearing five ruffles of green and white felt; three red roses and green leaves on her dress; matching green felt shoes.
MARKS: See page 126.

These two dolls are from Salvador in the Brazilian province of Bahia on the north Atlantic coast of Brazil. Here people of all nationalities and races live together in a nice climate. The deep water port is shown in the background.

216

216. *Left:* **Bahia Province Peddler Doll:** 18in (46cm); felt face mask with center seam only at back of head; heart-shaped mouth; black thread wig with side part; hands with a very large separate thumb; dressed in Bahai provincial costume; white rayon dress, apron and scarf; multi-colored felt appliqued on dress with fancy stitching; green pleated organdy trim around apron and bottom of skirt; blue cotton pants with blue felt trim; extra long legs; felt slippers with high heels; red rayon scarf; fruit in basket on head; wooden beads; brass earrings; circa 1930s.

MARKS: "Manufactura Orbis//Joao Perotti//S.Paulo//Industria Brasileire" on paper tag glued to underpants.

Right: **Bahia Girl in Original Box:** 13in (33cm); same general characteristics as the larger doll; red felt skirt with multi-colored felt pieces forming large flowers; blue rayon apron with the same type applique as the skirt; both skirt and apron have blue pleated organdy trim with felt borders; blue rayon blouse with puffed sleeves; pink scarf with red and blue yarn trim; red rayon scarf; fruit including bananas in straw basket on her head; wooden beads; brass earrings; wooden clogs with felt uppers; felt flowers on toes; circa 1930s.

MARKS: "Orbis//Original Bahiana on label on box with Brazilian Indian design. (The photograph in the background shows Salvador, a port in the coastal Province, Bahia.)

217. Perotti Girl in Provincial Outfit: 17in (43cm); 1930s; all felt; green and black wool fringed hat with blue band; black wool hair; two-tone red lips; mitt hands; wooden shoes with blue and orange felt tops decorated with sequins; multi-colored heavily embroidered dress and apron of velvet; black velvet jumper top; white rayon blouse with red rickrack trim; 1930s.
MARKS: "Joao Perotti//Re S.R. Alves de Lima...Sao Paulo//Made in Brazil" on tag sewn in dress.

217

218. Matador: 16in (41cm); semi-dark felt for face, hands, legs; no ears, painted face; red dots in corners of eyes; eyelashes above and below eyes; two-tone lips; embroidered black velvet pants and coat; red and black embroidered felt cape; black matador hat with pompons; 1920-1935.
MARKS: "Manufactura Orbis//Joao Perotti-St. Paulo//Industria Brazileira"

218

219. Native Craft Doll from Manaus: 11.5in (29cm); all reddish brown wood; wood burned **219** facial features and upper body decorations; native white feathers form the skirt; local beads form the feet; 1980s.

The background picture shows the colorful "Meeting of the Waters" near Manaus, Brazil. This unusual phenomenon takes place where the clear, dark waters of the Rio Negro River flow into the muddy brown waters of the Amazon River. For some distance downstream the two colors remain distinct. Visitors are taken to the floating craft workshops where floats are anchored together and many craft projects are made and sold in a "market-type economy. The doll pictured was made "on the river".

<u>MARKS</u>: None.

220. Brazilian Craft Doll: 10in (25cm); cardboard cone body and head; painted face; yarn hair; dress and umbrella are made from stiffened burlap; blue ribbon 1986. (The doll was purchased at a craft show in Rio de Janeiro, shown in the background photograph.) <u>MARKS</u>: None.

220

221

221. Brazilian Bride: 20in (51cm); Brazilian hard plastic head and limbs; crier; Brazilian cloth body; long, voluminous white wedding dress and veil.
<u>MARKS:</u> "Estrela//Amarca da//Sua Garantlia//os mais finosa Brinquedos//do Brazil" stamped on teddy, body and tag.
Sandi Dodd Collection.

222. Brazilian Costume Doll:
7.5in (19cm); composition; molded hair; painted face; jointed neck, shoulders, legs; white blouse with orange trim; black velvet and blue and white striped cotton jumper with crocheted trim; white oilcloth shoes; 1940s-1950s.(Note: This is a "Ginny-Type" doll from Estrela, a Brazilian doll company.)
MARKS: "Estrela//A Marca Da//Sua Garantia//As Mais Finosa Bomecas do//Brazil."

221

223. Brazilian Gaucho (Cowboy of the Brazilian Grasslands)**:** 18in (46cm); pressed felt mask; no ears; hand painted face; heart-shaped lips; felt wig; blue gaucho pants tucked into black boots with wooden high heels; multicolored checked shirt; red silk scarf around neck; leather belt; silver buckle; large metal medallions hanging down on belt extensions; white felt poncho over shoulder with intricate felt trim; black felt gaucho hat.
MARKS: "Joao Perotti//Joao Alves de Lima, 309/S.Paulo Ind. Brasileira" on paper tag glued to felt belt.

223

224. *Left to Right:* **Man:** 15in (38cm); stuffed cloth; embroidered facial features; feather quill fingernails; cotton twill striped suit; matching hat; flannel hair; shoes sewn to body; anatomically correct. **Lady:** 14in (36cm); stuffed cloth; embroidered facial features; feather quill fingernails; large legs; peach print skirt with blue cotton lace trim; yellow bodice and apron; blue turban; foil twisted to resemble jewelry. **Lady:** 14in (36cm); stuffed body; embroidered facial features; feather quill fingernails; blue silk faille dress; metallic ribbon; lace blouse; excellent detailing on costume; no accurate date, but the dolls are very old.
MARKS: "Rio-de Janerio//Made at Be-yo.ha//near the equator."
Joseph Colembieski Collection.

224

CHILE

Chile is almost 2,700 miles long and averages 110 miles wide and occupies the Pacific side of southern South America. The word "Chile" comes from an Indian word meaning "end of the earth." The European culture dominates Chile because of past immigration.

The "National Dance" of Chile is the Cueca, which is the vigorous handkerchief dance. It simulates the courtship of the rooster and hen. The traditional fabric of Chile is called *crin,* which is made from the roots of trees. A set of three crin nesting dolls dyed green and dancing the Cueca is often brought home by the tourists. The Chilean *huaso* is similar to an Argentinian gaucho. A *huasa* is his lady. Their typical clothing is found in rural areas.

225. Couple Dancing the Cueca: 7.5in (19cm) Lady; 9in (23cm) Man; cloth over wire; lady is holding the handkerchief; man wears a typical hat of Chile.
MARKS: "Garbep, S.A."

225

226. Huaso: 8in (20cm); Chilean cowboy; wears a short version of a red poncho, called a *manta* which is trimmed with blue; black cowboy pants with brown fringe on the side; white handkerchief; boots with silver spurs. **Huaso Lady:** 8in (20cm); black linen-like short jacket and long skirt trimmed with lace; white cotton blouse; lace handkerchief in pocket. Both dolls purchased through Kimport in 1943. **MARKS:** "Chile" banner on both dolls.
Shirley Karaba Collection.

226

227. Cueca Dancers: 10in (25cm); wooden heads, arms, hands, legs, and feet; wire bodies covered with cloth; painted faces; wool hair; man has a black felt hat with a string that has a bead to tighten it under the chin; white cotton shirt; beige cotton long pants with long sleeve vest to match; red, white, blue, striped poncho trimmed in red with embroidered flowers; black leather boots with carved heels; tin silver spurs; hands have carved fingers holding a handkerchief. The lady wears a flowered, yellow dress trimmed with lace; white cotton slip; white apron; black shoes; holds a blue kerchief; 1987. **MARKS:** None.
Sherry Morgan Collection.

227

228. Chilean Couple Dancing the Cueca: 4in (10cm); cloth and floss wrapped over an armature; bark base; painted composition faces; black wool wigs; man wears a gray felt hat; large collar with geometric design; white, cotton bolero; brown and white checked shirt; oilcloth pants and shoes; woman wears a white cotton overblouse trimmed with lace; full, green cotton skirt; dolls wired to base. **MARKS:** "Chile" on bark base.

228

COLOMBIA

The ethnic past of Colombia is Native American, European and African. Spanish is the language of the people because Colombia was a Spanish colony for 300 years.

229. Dancer: 8.5in (22cm); hard plastic, movable arms and legs; black wool hair with wide plait on right side; two layers of lace collar; white blouse; black pleated skirt with multicolored stripes; pointed straw hat; flowers in her hand. **MARKS:** "MUNECA TIPICA//COLOMBIANA" on gold tag on wrist.

229

230. Mother and Daughter: 11in (28cm), 6in (15cm); hand knitted in brown wool; stuffed; embroidered faces; long, black, wool hair. **Mother:** white wool knitted cap and poncho with black designs; white linen pants; white wool sandals with black ties and straw soles. **Daughter:** white wool dress with red and purple designs; wool bows in hair; daughter holds clay pitcher and mother's hand; 1982. Mother was purchased in Bogotá; daughter was purchased in Cartagena. **MARKS:** None. *Sherry Morgan Collection.*

230

ECUADOR

Ecuador, which means "equator" in Spanish, sits astride the Equator on the Pacific Ocean.

The native costumes are similar to those in other South American countries. The men wear serapes. Women wear a rebozo to carry babies and purchases. The people of Ecuador love hats, and they sometimes attach one or more to the first hat and let them all hang down their back.

The hat is often white llama wool which retains its shape in the rain. Panama hats were invented in Ecuador and sold to neighboring countries. The citizens of Panama liked and wore them, and when Americans passing through the Panama Canal by boat on the way to the "gold rush" in California bought them, they called them "Panama hats."

231. Otavalo Indian Couple. Man: 5in (13cm); cloth over armature; hat made of glue-stiffened felt; painted face; red felt cape; white cotton shirt and pants; thread black wig with ponytail in back; painted brown shoes; slim stick for flute. **Woman:** 4.5in (10cm); cloth over armature; painted face; white slip with hand-crocheted lace; pink felt skirt; yellow cotton blouse with red trim; gray cotton shawl; 1960s. **MARKS:** "Ecuador" wood burned on wooden stand.

231

232. Peasants: 8in (20cm); head, hands, arms made of carved tagua nuts from coastal forests; heavy stuffed cloth bodies; nut is carved to look like hair.

The printed page between the couple is from the Kimport *Doll News* which was published periodically and told about new Kimport products: "Nita and Leon are poor Indians. But, they wear bright costumes to market. Nita has endless tasks spinning wool, tending children, making things to sell and tending the fruit and vegetables. Leon works in the market and on the

232

farm, but at night he plays his crude harp with others in the village... The peculiar Ecuadorian hat is made very heavy so the high wind does not blow it away... The Tagua nuts are naturally white and are used in the manufacturing of fine buttons."

MARKS: None.

233

233. Two Otavalo Women: *Left:* 10.5in (27cm); painted clay head; felt body; hard brown Otavalo hat; white petticoat with lace; heavy soft fleece underslip; black fleece overskirt with red embroidery around the bottom which is open at left side to show inner skirt; white blouse with intricate embroidery. Cloth baby carried in rebozo; embroidered hair; long pink dress with blue embroidery; straw hand-woven shoes.

MARKS: "Genuine Ecuadorian Doll//Made by Lilly Winter//Province of Otavalo."

Right: 6.5in (17cm); wooden body; cloth over wood painted face; leather hat; pink rebozo for baby; white shawl; purple felt skirt with gold rickrack trim open at side to show inner skirt; white blouse with blue rickrack; blue wood shoes; cloth baby carried in rebozo.

MARKS: "From Ecuador" on bottom of base.

GUYANA

Guyana , formerly British Guiana, became a Dutch possession in the 17th century, but sovereignty passed to Britian in 1815. Indentured servants from India soon outnumbered African slaves, and now Indians are the major ethnic group.

234. Hindu Woman from British Guiana: 6in (15cm); entire body was molded of gray Balta Gum; carved face with inset bead eyes; bright red mouth; large gold earrings; nose ring; brass bracelets on arms and one foot; light green flowered silk print long dress; white chiffon Hindu veil, 1959; a Kimport Import.
MARKS: "This doll was made in British Guiana"

234

PARAGUAY

Paraguay is one of the two inland countries of South America, but it has a network of rivers with access to the sea. Spanish is the official language of Paraguay, but many of the people speak Guarani, an ancient Indian tongue.

235. Lady in Straw Hat: 9in (23cm); body is yarn wound around armature; wooden head; embroidered wool skirt; white embroidered serape; hard straw hat with red ribbon and yellow flower.
MARKS: "Par..." on bottom of stand.
Pat Parton Collection.

235

PERU — LAND OF LEGENDS

The powerful Inca empire had its seat at Cuzco in the Andes and it covered most of Peru, Bolivia and Ecuador. Building on the achievements of the more than 800 years of Andean civilization, the Incas had a high level of skill in architecture, engineering, textiles, and social organization. This ended when the Spanish conquered in 1532. Peru became independent from Spain in 1824.

236

236. Lady with Flag: 11in (28cm); molded clay face; black wool hair; cloth doll; hand-woven clothes; cloth over cardboard hat; 1981.
MARKS: Kimport tag with "Lima Peru" printed on it.
Thelma Purvis Collection.

237. Peddler Boy: 9in (23cm); painted ceramic head; cloth body; carrying a load on his back; 1981.
MARKS: None.
Thelma Purvis Collection.

237

THE DROP SPINDLE

In the Altiplano, the high plains in both Peru and Bolivia, almost all of the women, many of the men, and some of the children carry a spindle as they attend to their tasks or go to market. The spindle spins yarn from the wool of the llama or alpaca. Then the yarn is dyed and woven into colorful material on hand looms that are strung between two trees. Many Peruvian dolls carry a spindle.

238. Peruvian Lady with Drop Spindle: 8in (20cm); molded clay face; cloth body; Cuzco-style hat; yellow shawl with multi-colored trim; black skirt with yellow stitching and rickrack trim; leather sandals; 1960.
MARKS: None.
Louise Schnell Collection.

238

239

239. Lady Carnival Doll: 16in (41cm); stockinette body; blue lace blouse; yellow skirt banded with black ribbon. The white, stiff fedora hat indicates she is wealthy. Most women can only afford a brown hat. This is still true today, and it is customary for a woman to wear a hat when she goes outside her house. **Man Carnival Doll:** 16in (41cm); heavy cotton body; leather mask; typical Peruvian Indian costume that is embroidered heavily; white striped shirt; embroidered blue, knit sweater; hand woven, multicolored poncho made from llama wool; black pants with embroidery, knit sweater; llama wool shoes.

Carnival in Peru used to be celebrated with a grand parade, floats, dancing in the streets, and uninhibited excitement, however, the holiday turned from what was supposed to be a religious celebration to a wild out-of-control rampage, and people were hurt and even killed. The celebration is now prohibited.

These dolls were purchased from an antique shop in Peru in 1983, and they were made during the time of the old ways.
MARKS: None.

The Incas settled in this rough mountain land many years before the Europeans came to Peru. They painfully built terraces which could be tilled and provide them with food. Their ancestors, today, still use them.

240. *Left to Right:* **Indian Woman with Drop Spindle:** 7in (18cm); molded clay head; wire armature body with tan yarn carefully wound around it; red hat is holdover from ancient Indian tradition and worn by the women and men of the Cuzco area; hat is worn over a knitted skullcap which ties at the chin; the inside of the hat has an Inca design on a black lining; hand-woven blue skirt with bands of yellow, red, and white yarn; green hand-woven rebosa (shawl) with baby peeping out; carrying a drop spindle to make yarn as she walks; 1980. **Indian Woman with Clay Pot:** 7in (18cm); same costume as worn by the doll on left with different colors. 1980.
MARKS: None.

Village Mayor: 10in (25cm); molded, clay head; Cuzco-type hat; all-clothes hand-woven; white shirt; red wool shawl with yellow and green trim; black wool pants; holds a silver and black walking stick.

The mayors and other officials gather each Sunday morning for mass in this same costume. It is a spectacle for both the people of the area and also the tourists who come to this area of Peru. (The background photographs shows a terraced hillside used for agriculture dating back to Inca times.)
MARKS: None.

240

241. German composition doll wearing a doll dress sold at a typical market in the mountains of Peru. This dress was purchased from a peddler who approached a tour bus during a stop at a busy market. The hand-woven material in shades of red, yellow, green, pink, white, and black has bands of hand-woven tape sewn on the skirt. The shawl is pulled up around the doll's head to show the embroidery; 1980.
MARKS: None.

241

142

242

242. Peruvian Family: The picture in the background shows the barren Altiplano high up in the mountains of Peru and a real Peruvian mother and children resting with their llamas. The mother is wearing the brown fedora-type hat of the Peruvians. On one side of the picture is a toy llama. On the other side is a Bolivian mother and child doll. She wears the bowler-type hat of the Bolivian women. (The author uses this picture and doll to show the two types of hats.)
MARKS: None on llama dolls.

243. Mayors or Officials: 11in (28cm); and 9in (23cm); clay heads, hands, legs; cloth over armature body; Cuzco-type hats; homespun red sweaters with multi-colored embroidery; black homespun pants; white shirts; staff of office carried by Mayors. (Between the dolls is a storage jar, a reproduction of an antique from a museum in Peru.)
MARKS (on dolls): None.

243

244. Peruvian Burial Dolls: 10in (25cm); old hand-woven grave materials are used for dolls and for clothing, made of fine "net-like" material which is decaying; hand embroidered faces on both dolls.

There has been much written about the age of these dolls in doll publications, and there seems to be no final theory or answer about how old they are. The authors have been to Peru and have seen cloth that was very old. The reported graves are in a section of Peru which is extremely dry, and cloth does not deteriorate as it would in other climates. For years there have been reports of people in the streets of Lima and around the grave area selling the dolls to sailors, tourists, doll collectors, etc. who visit Peru; however, it is difficult and expensive to authenticate these dolls. When the authors acquired these dolls in July 1987, the sales slip said, "These dolls are called Inca Burial Dolls. Made by the Inca Indians in Peru, South America for their children to play with—made out of mummy cloth—about 1000 years old. Until they are authenticated, the authors feel that they are different, interesting handmade Peruvian dolls, no matter what their age.
MARKS: None.

244

URUGUAY

By 1624 the indigenous Charrua Indians were replaced by Spanish settlers in Uruguay. These and other immigrants from Portuguese Brazil and from Italy have become the majority. From Independence in 1825 until the late 1960s Uruguay's standard of living was one of the highest in South America. Strikes, terrorist activity and military control have changed all that.

245. *Left:* **Gauchito:** 8in (20cm); stockinette black felt gaucho hat with white band underneath; white neckerchief; blue wool bolero jacket edged in lighter blue wool worn over a white shirt; divided *chiripa* (baggy pants) edged with the same lighter blue which reaches from the waist to the calf; broad leather belt; white pants with lace at bottom; boots with low heels because the cattle land is flat, and the gaucho is forced to stand in the saddle to scan for distances; traditional fringed blanket over left shoulder; painted face with mustache; black wool hair; July 1956.
MARKS: "Gauchito Uruguayo" stamped in leather on the bottom of the stand which is covered with imitation grass to imitate the Pampas.

Right: **Gauchito:** 10in (25cm); molded clay face with mustache; wide brimmed gaucho hat with no white band underneath, which is a newer fashion; white taffeta shirt; blue

245 knotted scarf; leather bolero jacket with rose cross stitches embroidered on it; divided *chiripa* edged with white trim; high white leather boots with spurs; black leather belt with silver ornament; bolo balls for leather thong to trip the cattle instead of lassoing them.
MARKS: "Made in Uruguay" on piece of a log used for a base; 1970s. From Kimport Dolls. (Note: "Gauchito" means "little Gaucho" or "Gaucho doll.")

144

VENEZUELA

Columbus first set foot on the South American continent on the peninsula of Paria in August of 1498. Venezuela was under Spanish domination until 1821. The oil discoveries of 1917 greatly aided the economy until the severe crisis of the 1980s and 1990s from falling oil revenues.

246. Venezuelan Girl Dancing the Yarn Dance: 6in (15cm); hard vinyl face and hands; high red hat; multi-colored striped shawl; white blouse; striped multicolored shirt; yarn balls for dance; 1980. (This doll shows a traditional dance of a betrothed Venezuelan girl. She is dancing for coins for her dowry.)
MARKS: None.
Thelma Purvis Collection.

246

247

247. Diablo: 5.5in (14cm); felt over armature body; colorful doll with red felt basic costume; orange cross on chest; yellow felt face; felt patches for eyes, nose, mouth, eyebrows, ears; felt short black felt shoes; 1970s. (Diablo [the Devil] is a carnival figure, and there are similar dolls in many sizes from Venezuela.)
MARKS: "Diablo de Yare//Venezuela" on base.

Left: **Girl in National Costume:** 4in (10cm); vinyl head and arms; cloth body; costume has a salmon pink print pattern with scallops for the skirt and a traditional white lace blouse trimmed with scallops. In Venezuela a black lace mantilla completes the ensemble. The doll's black hair with braids and a pink rose on her forehead looks very much like a mantilla. The sandals on her feet are the right style with open toes. She is ready for the celebration called "The Day of the Liberator."
MARKS: "Llancera//Venezuela" on the base.

145

248. *Left:* **Woman in Red Dress:**
14in (36cm); all-cloth; dressed in
sophisticated red, gold and blue
dress; red hat; carrying large gold
bouquet. *Right:* **Stylized
Venezuelan Man:** 19in (48cm);
body entirely made of straw. These
two dolls were purchased in a
flower shop in 1980.
MARKS: None.
Thelma Purvis Collection.

248

249. *Left:* **Venezuelan Fertility
Doll:** 13in (33cm); hand-knit with
orange, red, purple, white and
black llama wool; two knitted
children in same colors attached
to dress. *Right:* **Venezuelan
Fertility Doll:** Woman knitted
with white, gray and black llama
wool; two knitted children in
same colors attached to dress;
purchased in Caracas, Venezuela;
1984.
MARKS: None.
Thelma Purvis Collection.

249

PRICE GUIDE

Illustration #	Description	Price	I Want	I Have
1	Widgeon, a Lubra Aborigine in the Australian Outback	$40-50	❏	❏
2	English Man Criminal Sent to Australia as Penalty	30-35	❏	❏
2	English Woman Criminal Sent to Australia	30-35	❏	❏
3	Koala Dressed as a Swagman	25-30	❏	❏
3	Budgerree Doll (Aborigine Warrior Chief)	85-110	❏	❏
3	Kangaroo with a Baby in her Pouch	15-20	❏	❏
4	Three Swaggies	25-50 ea.	❏	❏
5	Early Settler of Australia	25-30	❏	❏
6	Aboriginal Couple from Australia	15-18	❏	❏
7	Bindi	35-45	❏	❏
8	Aboriginal	30-40	❏	❏
9	Maori Mother and Baby	40-60	❏	❏
9	Maori Dancer	N/A	❏	❏
10	Maori Toddler Hemi	550+	❏	❏
11	Wahine	50-75	❏	❏
11	Warrior	50-75	❏	❏
12	Piu Skirt Dolls	40-60	❏	❏
13	Pania	50-75	❏	❏
13	Authentic Wahine	40-75	❏	❏
14	Mira Maoriland's Maid	50-75	❏	❏
15	Authentic Wahine Dancer	50-75	❏	❏
16	Fruit Peddler (Antigua)	12-15	❏	❏
17	Fruit Peddler (Aruba)	25-50	❏	❏
18	Abaco Island Bahamas Policeman	20-30	❏	❏
19	Raffia Clown	8-10	❏	❏
19	Bermuda Policeman	20-30	❏	❏
20	Man Playing Steel Drum	25-35	❏	❏
21	Bermuda Lady	20-25	❏	❏
22	Fidel Castro	90-100	❏	❏
23	Cuban Dancers	15-25	❏	❏
24	Two Dancers in Cuban Nightclub	40-50 ea.	❏	❏
25	Island Woman	12-18	❏	❏
26	Peddler Pushing a Cart	20-25	❏	❏
27	Man from Puerta Plata	20-25	❏	❏
27	Lady in Ribbon Dress	25-30	❏	❏
28	Man and Woman	10 ea.	❏	❏
28	Paris Court Lady	N/A	❏	❏
29	Peddler Dolls —Woman	20-25	❏	❏

Instances where more than one doll is presented in description ea. marks price for each.
*Few prices available. **At Auction.*

Illustration #	Description	Price	I Want	I Have
29	Man	$15-20	❏	❏
30	Limbo Dancer	50-75	❏	❏
31	Traditional Jamaican Lady Doll	20-25	❏	❏
31	Mother Sitting with Baby	20-25	❏	❏
31	Boy Playing a Ukulele	20-25	❏	❏
32	Man and Woman	20-25	❏	❏
32	Girl Dressed in Martinique Costume	25-30	❏	❏
33	Fashion Lady	65-75	❏	❏
34	Martinique Fashion Lady	65-75	❏	❏
35	Maid and Baby in Colonial Days	15-20	❏	❏
36	Banana Cutter Man	40-60	❏	❏
37	Puerto Rican Girl with Basket and Guitar	25-35	❏	❏
38	Dancing Girl with Gourds	5-10	❏	❏
38	Two Man Band	10-15	❏	❏
39	Topsy Turvy Upside Down Dolls	25-30	❏	❏
40	Brimstone Hill Fort Pirate	35-45	❏	❏
41	St. Lucia Grande Dame	15-18	❏	❏
41	Nassau Child	15-18	❏	❏
42	Man with Red Drum from St. Maarten	20-25	❏	❏
42	Man with Striped Drum	14-20	❏	❏
43	Chiquita Doll	15-20	❏	❏
44	St. John, Virgin Islands Family	45-65	❏	❏
45	Two Indian Women	30 ea.	❏	❏
46	Coffee Picker	30-40	❏	❏
47	Wood Peddler	25-35	❏	❏
47	Ecuador Girl	25-35	❏	❏
48-49	Man with Votive Box	40-60	❏	❏
50	Guatemalan Peddlers	55-65 all	❏	❏
51	Guatemalan Couple Coming Home From Market	20-25	❏	❏
52	Woman Carrying Vegetables on Head	25-30	❏	❏
52	Peddler Man	25-30	❏	❏
52	Musician	25-35	❏	❏
53	Woman Peddler	25-30	❏	❏
54	Guatemalan Musicians	25-35	❏	❏
55	Tiny Doll Family	25-30	❏	❏
56	Honduran Good Luck Girl	12-18	❏	❏
57	Nela of Nicaragua	30-40	❏	❏
58	Straw Doll	15-20	❏	❏
59	Man in Embroidered Suit	25-35	❏	❏
60	Doll Dressed in Pollera Costume	50-75	❏	❏

*Few prices available. **At Auction.*

Illustration #	Description	Price	I Want	I Have
61	Horn Doll	$300-400	❏	❏
62	Native American (Alaskan) Couple w/Baby & Dog Team	100-150	❏	❏
63	Nuni Doll Holding Snowballs	70-80	❏	❏
63	Doll with Carved Hair	100-150	❏	❏
63	Sillikens	15-20	❏	❏
63	Lady with yellow clothes	*	❏	❏
64	Shot-Kee-Doh	35-50	❏	❏
65	Alaskan Native American	*	❏	❏
66	Fairbanks Native American Couple	*	❏	❏
67	Alaskan Native Fisherman	*	❏	❏
68	Alaskan Tlingit Native American	*	❏	❏
68	South Dakota Oglala Sioux Eagle Dancer	*	❏	❏
69	Alaskan Native	*	❏	❏
69	Nuni	90-150	❏	❏
69	Smanisse Norwegian Native Doll	N/A	❏	❏
70	Nuni (Kiana) Doll	90-150	❏	❏
70	Original Naber Zipper Pullcord Doll	500-800	❏	❏
71	Eric	200-300	❏	❏
71	Natasha	200-300	❏	❏
71	Kilo (Baby)	*	❏	❏
71	Sissi Face	1,000-1,800	❏	❏
72	Northwest Territories Canadian Native	30-50	❏	❏
72	Alaskan Aleut Eskimo Woman	*	❏	❏
72	Alaskan Kuskokwim	60-70	❏	❏
73	Old Man	400-500	❏	❏
74	Alberta Province Assiniboine Tribe Doll	45-55	❏	❏
74	Quebec Province Iroquois Tribe Doll in Crawling Position	70-90	❏	❏
74	Alberta Stoney or Assiniboine Doll	100-125	❏	❏
75	Quebec Province Inuit Native Canadian on Ice Fishing for a Seal	75-100	❏	❏
75	Province of Ontario Native Canadians	50-75	❏	❏
76	Quebec Native Canadian	40-50	❏	❏
77	Canadian Native	*	❏	❏
77	Bone Doll	100-125	❏	❏
77	Old Woman	*	❏	❏
78	Native Canadian	*	❏	❏
79	Native Girl in Fringed Skin Dress and Hair Band	N/A	❏	❏
79	Native Canadian Girl in Dark Blue Skin Dress	N/A	❏	❏
79	Native Canadian in Pink Short Leather Fringed Dress	20-25	❏	❏
80	Canadian Native Squaw	150-170	❏	❏

*Few prices available. **At Auction.

Illustration #	Description	Price	I Want	I Have
81	Huron Native Canadian Doll	$75-80	❏	❏
81	Huron Canadian Dolls (3)	50-70 ea.	❏	❏
82	Native Canadian	50-100	❏	❏
83	Native Canadian Boy	50-75	❏	❏
84	Native Canadian	25-30	❏	❏
84	Native Canadian Doll	50-75	❏	❏
85	Native Canadian Doll	75-100	❏	❏
86	Native Canadian Girl	N/A	❏	❏
87	Royal Canadian Mounted Police	50-75	❏	❏
87	Royal Canadian Mounted Police	250-300	❏	❏
88	Anne of Green Gables	50-70	❏	❏
89	Girl Guide	250-300	❏	❏
90	Boy and Girl	15-20	❏	❏
91	Poblana of Puebla	50-60	❏	❏
92	Man Playing Harp	30-40	❏	❏
93	China Girl	150-175	❏	❏
94	Charro (Gentleman Horseman)	100-125	❏	❏
95	Three Mexican Costumed Dolls	20-25 ea.	❏	❏
95	Girl with Red Print Headscarf and Bodice	20-25	❏	❏
95	Boy with Decorated Charro Suit	20-29	❏	❏
95	Tehuacán Girl Wearing Variation of Huipil Costume	20-25	❏	❏
96	Dance of the Three Old Men	50-75	❏	❏
97	Bride and Groom Dressed in Michoacán Tradition	85-100	❏	❏
98	Feather Dancer	25-30	❏	❏
99	Mexican Corn Grinder Doll	15-25	❏	❏
99	Charro (Gentleman Horseman)	100-125	❏	❏
100	Pineapple Man and Woman	10 ea.	❏	❏
101	Santa Claus with Umbrella and Bell	25-35	❏	❏
101	Basket Scene of Children Breaking Piñata	20-30	❏	❏
102	Donkey Piñata	6-10	❏	❏
102	Feather Dancer	5-8	❏	❏
102	Pink and Green Strawman	8-12	❏	❏
103	Feathered Aztec Dolls	10-20	❏	❏
104	Mexican Bullfighter	N/A	❏	❏
105	Strawman	5-10	❏	❏
106	Tehuacán Girl Wearing Native Costume	20-35	❏	❏
106	Doll in China Costume	20-35	❏	❏
107	Aztec Lady	50-55	❏	❏
108	Mexican Lady	120-130	❏	❏
109	Margaret Blennerhasset	20-25	❏	❏

*Few prices available. **At Auction.*

Illustration #	Description	Price	I Want	I Have
110	Early Football Player (13in)	$50-80	❑	❑
110	Early Football Player (4.5in)	15-25	❑	❑
111	Nut-Head Doll	5-10	❑	❑
112	Southern Gentlemen	15-20	❑	❑
113	Corn Husk Dolls	3-20 ea.	❑	❑
113	Lady with Red Hair Wearing an Apron and Scarf with Multicolored Stars	15-20	❑	❑
113	Child Carrying Flowers	N/A	❑	❑
113	Mother Holding the Hand of Her Child (corncob)	12-18	❑	❑
113	Child with Red Pigtails Holding Flowers	1-15	❑	❑
113	Mother with Red Hair Holding a Baby in Her Arms	1-15	❑	❑
113	Child Holding a Doll	1-15	❑	❑
113	Woman Sitting on a Bench Spinning	1-15	❑	❑
113	Young Lady Pushing a Doll in a Small Cart	1-15	❑	❑
113	Child Dressed Up Like Mother Carrying a Broom	1-20	❑	❑
113	Mother Sitting on a Bench Spanking Her Son	1-15	❑	❑
113	Child on Top of a Slide	1-15	❑	❑
114	Pioneer-type Dolls	15-20	❑	❑
114	Cornhusk American Woman/Baby	15-20/1-15	❑	❑
114	American Applehead Doll	12-18	❑	❑
114	Pioneer Corncob Mother and Baby	12-18	❑	❑
115	Selling Vegetables in Dixie	15-20	❑	❑
116	Casquette Girl	65-85	❑	❑
117	Mardi Gras Clown	10-15	❑	❑
118	Amish Dolls	15-20	❑	❑
118	Father	15-20	❑	❑
118	Mother	15-20	❑	❑
118	Children	5-10	❑	❑
119	Pilgrim	10-15	❑	❑
119	Indian Girl	2-5	❑	❑
119	Girl in Center	2-5	❑	❑
119	Small Carved Wooden Pilgrim Pair	5-10	❑	❑
119	Carved Wooden Indian	5-10	❑	❑
119	Pilgrim Man and Woman	5-10	❑	❑
119	Mohawk Boy with Pointed Haircut	8-10	❑	❑
119	Pilgrim Lady	10-15	❑	❑
120	Northern Civil War Soldier (hard-to-find)	25-35	❑	❑
121	Confederate Soldier (hard-to-find)	25-35	❑	❑
122	General Robert E. Lee (hard-to-find)	25-35	❑	❑
122	General Ulysses S. Grant (hard-to-find)	25-35	❑	❑

*Few prices available. **At Auction.

Illustration #	Description	Price	I Want	I Have
122	Soldier	$25-45	❏	❏
123	Aviator	500-800	❏	❏
124	Marie Laveau	125-150	❏	❏
124	Voodoo Doll	8-10	❏	❏
125	Baby in Cradle	80-100	❏	❏
125	Squaw with Baby	N/A	❏	❏
125	Squaw	N/A	❏	❏
126	Navaho Native American Dolls from Colorado	20-30	❏	❏
127	Paiute Baby on Cradleboard	160-200	❏	❏
127	South Dakota Sioux Native American	60-75	❏	❏
128	Cherokee Doll on Trail of Tears	80-100	❏	❏
129	Kathleen Sioux	400	❏	❏
129	Buckskin Doll	85-95	❏	❏
130	Native American Storyteller (5in)	45-50	❏	❏
131	Native American Storyteller (17.5in)	25-50	❏	❏
132	Ten Seminoles from Florida	20-50	❏	❏
132	Three Small Wooden Kachinas	N/A	❏	❏
132	One Large Kachina	50-70	❏	❏
132	Alaskan Aladeau	35-45	❏	❏
132	Leather Native American Woman	*	❏	❏
132	Three Carved Wood Native Americans	145	❏	❏
133	Seminole Woman from Florida	50-70	❏	❏
134	North Carolina Cherokees	20-25 ea.	❏	❏
134	Squaw	20-25	❏	❏
134	Squaw	20-25	❏	❏
135	Old Sioux Doll	2,900**	❏	❏
136	St. Regis Corn Dancer	15-200	❏	❏
137	Hopi Kachinas	125-150	❏	❏
138	Kachina Dolls	N/A	❏	❏
139	Nez Perce Princess from Sandy Doll Co.	65-75	❏	❏
140	Shoshoni Indian Dancer	50-100	❏	❏
141	Native Americans: Arctic	135-150	❏	❏
141	Canadian Yukon	N/A	❏	❏
141	Arctic	*	❏	❏
141	Canadian Arctic	*	❏	❏
141	Cherokee Woman from Georgia	N/A	❏	❏
141	Group of Totem Poles from the Northwest	Varies	❏	❏
141	Papoose	*	❏	❏
141	Woman and Men Cheyenne from Colorado	50-60 ea.	❏	❏
141	Huron from Ontario	49-60 ea.	❏	❏

*Few prices available. **At Auction.*

Illustration #	Description	Price	I Want	I Have
141	Eagle Dancer from Kiowa Tribe	$89-100	❑	❑
142	Navaho Woman (14in)	30	❑	❑
142	Navaho Woman (11in)	35	❑	❑
142	Teepee with Symbol for Man	35	❑	❑
142	Celluloid Native American	20-30	❑	❑
142	Stylized Cloth Native American Woman	25	❑	❑
143	Falling Snow	N/A	❑	❑
143	Sioux Burial Doll	250-400	❑	❑
144	Makah from Neah Bay, Washington	50-75	❑	❑
144	Montana Blackfoot Indian	45-60	❑	❑
145	Washington State Makah Woman and Man	300+ pair	❑	❑
146	Navaho Native American Loom Doll	50-80	❑	❑
147	Skookum Apple Doll	175-225	❑	❑
148	Pottery Head	N/A	❑	❑
149	Adena Pipe	N/A	❑	❑
150	Eagle Kachina	200-150	❑	❑
151	Owl Kachina	*	❑	❑
152	Navajo Sand Painter	Rare*	❑	❑
153	Indian Boy Key Chain	5-10	❑	❑
154	First Wind, Pawnee Woman	N/A	❑	❑
154	Apache Tribe White Eagle	N/A	❑	❑
155	Wyoming Shoshone	N/A	❑	❑
155	Sitting Doll	30-50	❑	❑
155	Couple	125	❑	❑
156	Texas Native American Man and Wife	70-80 pair	❑	❑
157	Frontier Trapper	40-50	❑	❑
158	Clapper Doll	30-35	❑	❑
159	American Cowboy	90-100	❑	❑
160	Arkansas Traveler	10-15	❑	❑
161	Civil War-type Doll	1-5	❑	❑
162	Sugar Time Man	20-30	❑	❑
163	Coast Guard Cadet	7-10	❑	❑
164	West Point Cadet	10-15	❑	❑
165-166	Tapa cloth dolls	N/A	❑	❑
167	Fiji Policeman	60-80	❑	❑
168	Lady Doll	20-25	❑	❑
169	Huapala Doll	20-30	❑	❑
170	Hawaiian Shimmy Doll	40-50	❑	❑
171	Early Missionary, Mrs. Baldwin, a Doctor's Wife	20-25	❑	❑
172	Kechi-Iki (Tiny baby)	8-15	❑	❑

*Few prices available.   **At Auction.

Illustration #	Description	Price	I Want	I Have
173	Chief and Lady	*	❏	❏
174	Boy and Girl Flat Wooden Dolls in Wooden Basket (price includes Kukane's & Nani's Clothes	$70-100	❏	❏
175	Hula Doll	100-150	❏	❏
176	Hawaiian Princess Doll from Big Island of Hawaii	100-150	❏	❏
177	Young Girl in Holom'u	15-18	❏	❏
178	Tutu Muumuu Grandmother	35-45	❏	❏
179	Small Hula Dancer	15-20	❏	❏
179	Large Hula Dancer	15-20	❏	❏
179	Hawaiian Kisses	50-75	❏	❏
180	Haleloke with Wardrobe in Trunk	250-300	❏	❏
181	Carved Wood Hawaiian Girl	400-450	❏	❏
182	Dancer (7in)	15-20 pair	❏	❏
182	Hula Dancer	10-15	❏	❏
182	Musical Dancer	40-50	❏	❏
182	Shimmy Dancer (6in)	15-20	❏	❏
183	Lady	25-35	❏	❏
184	New Guinea Lady	50-60	❏	❏
185	New Guinea Wolf Ceremonial Flute	N/A	❏	❏
186	Dancing the Tinkling	20-25	❏	❏
186	Bride	40-50+	❏	❏
187	Moros Couple	40-50	❏	❏
188	Lady	20-30	❏	❏
188	Peddler	20-30	❏	❏
188	Man Pounding Grains	20-30	❏	❏
188	Peddler Woman	20-30	❏	❏
188	Peddler Man Selling Meals	20-30	❏	❏
188	Lady Shopper	N/A	❏	❏
189	Lady of Ilocano tribe	40-50	❏	❏
190	Negrito Man	50-70 Rare	❏	❏
191	Pitcairn Island Man	25-35	❏	❏
192	Hula Dancer from Pogo Pogo	25-35	❏	❏
193	Dancing Girl	30-40	❏	❏
194	Gaucho	75	❏	❏
194	Lady	75	❏	❏
195	Argentinian Cowboy	100-125	❏	❏
195	Small Boy Cowboy	35-45	❏	❏
196	Gaucho	400-500+	❏	❏
197	Indian	150-250	❏	❏
198	Gaucho	25-45	❏	❏

*Few prices available. **At Auction.*

Illustration #	Description	Price	I Want	I Have
199	Lencilandia Girl Carrying a Bunch of Peaches	N/A	❏	❏
200	Blonde Lady	$150-200	❏	❏
200	Brunette Lady	10-25	❏	❏
200	Lady with Bananas	N/A	❏	❏
201	Witch Doctor Market	8-10	❏	❏
202	Bolivian Peddler Doll	20-30	❏	❏
203	The Dolls of Lake Titicaca	20-25 ea.	❏	❏
204	Bolivian Wall Hanging	35-45	❏	❏
205	Boy Playing Flute	25-30	❏	❏
206	Man Playing Flute	30-35	❏	❏
206	Lady and Baby	30-35	❏	❏
207	Bolivian Dancer	40-50	❏	❏
207	Sucre Man	30-35	❏	❏
208	Masked Devil Dancer	40-45	❏	❏
209	Girl with Guitar	N/A	❏	❏
210	Theatre Carnival Dancer	N/A	❏	❏
211	Carnival Doll	N/A	❏	❏
212	Fruit Peddler (Brazil)	N/A	❏	❏
213	Brazilian Girl	N/A	❏	❏
214	Girl Carrying a Basket of Vegetables	N/A	❏	❏
215	Brazilian Peddler	400-500	❏	❏
215	Doll with Guitar	500-600	❏	❏
215	Little Girl	40-50	❏	❏
216	Bahia Province Peddler Doll	500-600	❏	❏
216	Bahia Girl in Original Box	500-600+	❏	❏
217	Perotti Girl in Provincial Outfit	500-600	❏	❏
218	Matador	700-800+	❏	❏
219	Native Craft Doll from Manaus	10-20	❏	❏
220	Brazilian Craft Doll	10-20	❏	❏
221	Brazilian Bride	250-300	❏	❏
222	Brazilian Costume Doll	35-55	❏	❏
223	Brazilian Gaucho	600-700	❏	❏
224	Man	*	❏	❏
224	Lady (14in)	*	❏	❏
224	Lady (14in)	*	❏	❏
225	Couple Dancing the Cueca	40-50	❏	❏
226	Huaso	250	❏	❏
226	Huaso Lady	250	❏	❏
227	Cueca Dancers	30-40	❏	❏
228	Chilean Couple Dancing the Cueca	5-10	❏	❏

*Few prices available. **At Auction.

Illustration #	Description	Price	I Want	I Have
229	Dancer	$30-40	❏	❏
230	Mother	15	❏	❏
230	Daughter	15	❏	❏
231	Otavalo Indian Man	10-12	❏	❏
231	Otavalo Indian Woman	10-12	❏	❏
232	Peasants	40-50	❏	❏
233	Two Otavalo Women	30-40	❏	❏
234	Hindu Woman from British Guiana RARE	45-60	❏	❏
235	Lady in Straw Hat	15-20	❏	❏
236	Lady with Flag	20-30	❏	❏
237	Peddler Boy	15-20	❏	❏
238	Peruvian Lady with Drop Spindle	12-15	❏	❏
239	Lady Carnival Doll	200-300	❏	❏
239	Man Carnival Doll	200-300	❏	❏
240	Indian Woman with Drop Spindle	25-30	❏	❏
240	Indian Woman with Clay Pot	N/A	❏	❏
240	Village Mayor	N/A	❏	❏
241	German Composition Doll	20-25	❏	❏
242	Llama	25-35	❏	❏
242	Peruvian Family	12-15	❏	❏
243	Mayors or Officials	30-40	❏	❏
244	Peruvian Burial Dolls	*	❏	❏
245	Gauchito (8in)	N/A	❏	❏
245	Gauchito (10in)	N/A	❏	❏
246	Venezuelan Girl Dancing the Yarn Dance	20-25	❏	❏
247	Diablo	15-25	❏	❏
247	Girl in National Costume	20-30	❏	❏
248	Woman in Red Dress	12-15	❏	❏
248	Stylized Venezuelan Man	10-18	❏	❏
249	Venezuelan Fertility Doll 13in (33cm)	10-18	❏	❏
249	Venezuelan Fertility Doll	10-18	❏	❏

*Few prices available. **At Auction.*

INDEX

157

ABOUT THE AUTHORS

Both mother and daughter enjoy collecting dolls and learning more about dolls as a team. It was understandable that their research efforts and their love of sharing doll information would progress from writing articles for the leading doll collector's magazines to a book. Their first book, *Hard Plastic Dolls, Volume I,* and the hundreds of letters of encouragement that they received started them on a dozen year odyssey of writing a total of ten books. Both skilled researchers, Polly says "It just came 'naturally' that my daughter, Pam, and I write about the hobby we enjoy so much – doll collecting."

A retired junior high school teacher and Coordinator for Chapter I Reading Program for the Wickliffe City Schools, Polly devotes most of her time to writing. Pam currently teaches fifth graders and is a performing harpsichordist with a Masters in Musicology. Both women reside in Ohio.

OTHER IDENTIFICATION & PRICE GUIDES BY THE JUDDS

HARD PLASTIC DOLLS, VOLUME I
An indispensible identification and price guide for every collector wanting to know more about hard plastic dolls of the 40s and 50s and their collectors' values. Over 600 photographs are combined with detailed descriptions to help the collector identify these dolls produced from 1946-1959. 312 pages. 5-1/2" x 8". PB. Item #H4638. $14.95

HARD PLASTIC DOLLS, VOLUME II
Learn about Alexander, American Character, Arranbee, Ideal, Nancy Ann, plus many more manufacturers! Discover how to identify hard plastic dolls by shoes and feet. 43 color plus 394 b/w photos. 256 pages. 5-1/2" x 8". PB. Item #H4703. $14.95

GLAMOUR DOLLS 1950s & 1960s
Featured are glamour dolls pictured in original costumes as well as many fabulous illustrations from vintage catalogs. Informs collectors of the characteristics of valuable glamour dolls. Over 400 photos. 256 pages. 5-1/2" x 8". PB. Item #H4639. $12.95

CLOTH DOLLS, 1920s & 1930s
Expansive photo guide to cloth dolls made by Lenci, Nora Welling, Chad Valley and many others. Lavishly illustrated with a bevy of beautiful photos plus packed with detailed descriptions to make identification simple. 47 color and 271 b/w photos. 256 pages. 5-1/2" x 8". PB. Item #H3979. $12.95

COMPOSITION DOLLS I, 1928-1955
A long-awaited, much needed guide to composition dolls aids collectors with those favorite postwar friends. 428 photographs display difficult-to-identify dolls augmented by a bevy of detailed text containing the most-up-to-date accurate values. An indispensable book for modern doll collectors. 130 color and 298 b/w photos. 8-1/2" x 11". HB. Item #H4389. $29.95

COMPOSITION DOLLS II, 1909-1928
Featuring the early prewar character dolls of 1909-1928, Volume II is the companion to Volume I. 302 photographs display difficult-to-identify dolls. Information is dedicated to the marks, characteristics and company stories of both the small and large manufacturers. Latest values. 135 color and 167 b/w photos. 176 pages. 8-1/2" x 11". HB. Item #H4691. $25.00

SANTA DOLLS & FIGURINES PRICE GUIDE:
ANTIQUE TO CONTEMPORARY, *REVISED EDITION*
Discover valuable information about your favorite Santa collectibles from the information and price guide as well as the legends of Gift-Givers from other countries. Enjoy the different styles of Santa dolls, figurines, paper dolls and post cards and their costumes in 121 gorgeous color photographs and 146 b/w photographs. 160 pages. 5-1/2" x 8". PB. Item #H4702. $14.95

EUROPEAN COSTUMED DOLLS
The definitive price and identification guide for costume or travel dolls of Europe. The first book of a series. With 250 photos (over half in color) you will be able to identify costume styles and see the beauty of the unique European costume Dolls. These dolls are appreciating in value as people focus on their ancestry! Fascinating historical and cultural information. 160 pages. 6" x 9". PB. Item #H4741. $14.95

AFRICAN AND ASIAN COSTUMED DOLLS
Definitive price and identification guide for costumed and travel dolls of Africa and Asia! 250 Photographs aid in identifying these sought after dolls. Fascinating historical and cultural information. Second in a series by Polly and Pam Judd. The first was *European Costumed Dolls.* 176 pages. 6" x 9". PB. Item #H4947. $14.95

Call 1-800-554-1447 to order.